Augsburg Commentary on the New Testament

EPHESIANS
Walter F. Taylor Jr.

COLOSSIANS
John H. P. Reumann

Augsburg Publishing House
Minneapolis, Minnesota

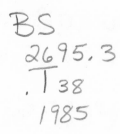

AUGSBURG COMMENTARY ON THE NEW TESTAMENT
Ephesians, Colossians

Scripture quotations unless otherwise noted are from the Revised Standard Version of the Bible, copyright 1946, 1952, and 1971 by the Division of Christian
Education of the National Council of Churches.

Library of Congress Cataloging-in-Publication Data

Reumann, John Henry Paul.
  COLOSSIANS.

  (Augsburg Commentary on the New Testament)
  Includes bibliographies.
  1. Bible. N.T. Ephesians—Commentaries.   2. Bible.
N.T. Colossians—Commentaries.   I. Taylor, Walter F.,
1946-   . Ephesians. 1985.   II. Title.   III. Title:
Ephesians.   IV. Series.
BS2695.3.T38 1985   227'.507   85-7479
ISBN 0-8066-2165-6

Manufactured in the U.S.A.   APH 10-9030

1   2   3   4   5   6   7   8   9   0   1   2   3   4   5   6   7   8   9

CONTENTS

ABBREVIATIONS

CD	Damascus Document (from the Dead Sea Scrolls)
CTM	*Currents in Theology and Mission*
IDB	*The Interpreter's Dictionary of the Bible*
IDBS	*The Interpreter's Dictionary of the Bible, Supplementary Volume*
JB	The Jerusalem Bible
JBL	*Journal of Biblical Literature*
KJV	King James Version
LBW	*Lutheran Book of Worship*
LXX	Septuagint (Greek OT)
Moffatt	*The New Testament*, trans. James Moffatt
NAB	The New American Bible
NEB	The New English Bible
NT	New Testament
NIV	The New International Version
NTS	*New Testament Studies*
OT	Old Testament
Phillips	*The New Testament in Modern English*, trans. J. B. Phillips
1QH	Thanksgiving Hymns (from the Dead Sea Scrolls)
1QS	Manual of Discipline (from the Dead Sea Scrolls)
RSR	*Religious Studies Review*
RSV	Revised Standard Version
SNTSMS	Society for New Testament Studies Monograph Series
TEV	Today's English Version (The Good News Bible)

FOREWORD

The AUGSBURG COMMENTARY ON THE NEW TESTA-
MENT is written for laypeople, students, and pastors. Laypeople
will use it as a resource for Bible study at home and at church.
Students and instructors will read it to probe the basic message
of the books of the New Testament. And pastors will find it to
be a valuable aid for sermon and lesson preparation.

The plan of each commentary is designed to enhance its use-
fulness. The Introduction presents a topical overview of the biblical book to be discussed and provides information on the
historical circumstances in which that book was written. It may
also contain a summary of the biblical writer's thought. In the
body of the commentary, the interpreter sets forth in brief com-
pass the meaning of the biblical text. The procedure is to explain
the text section by section. Care has also been taken to avoid the
heavy use of technical terms. Because the readers of the commentary will have their Bibles at hand, the biblical text itself has
not been printed out. In general, the editors recommend the use
of the Revised Standard Version of the Bible.

The authors of this commentary series are professors at sem-
inaries and universities and are themselves ordained. They have
been selected both because of their expertise and because they

worship in the same congregations as the people for whom they are writing. In elucidating the text of Scripture, therefore, they attest to their belief that central to the faith and life of the church of God is the Word of God.

The Editorial Committee

Roy A. Harrisville
Luther Northwestern Theological Seminary
St. Paul, Minnesota

Jack Dean Kingsbury
Union Theological Seminary
Richmond, Virginia

Gerhard A. Krodel
Lutheran Theological Seminary
Gettysburg, Pennsylvania

EPHESIANS

Walter F. Taylor Jr.

Rev. C. Willard Carlson, 1914–1978
In Memoriam
He spoke "the truth in love" (Eph. 4:15)

INTRODUCTION TO EPHESIANS

It is hard to touch anything in Ephesians without encountering—or creating—a problem. Virtually every aspect of the standard list of introductory questions seems up for grabs. Twentieth-century scholarship has "determined" that Ephesians was written by Paul, by Onesimus, by Luke, or by an unknown disciple. It was written to Ephesus, to several congregations in Asia Minor, or to an unknown congregation or congregations. It was written in the 50s or 60s of the first century—or in the 90s or later. It is a baptismal treatise, written to establish Paul's authority, written to introduce his letters, or we do not know why it was written. It has clear affinities with the Dead Sea Scrolls; it uses Gnostic language to combat the Gnostics, it is a Gnostic document, it shows no knowledge of Gnosticism at all. It " . . . has been seen as the mature fruit of Paul's thought, as the beginning of its distortion, or as an inspired reinterpretation."[1] Other than these small matters, everything about Ephesians is crystal clear!

It is the task of the introduction to seek to bring some preliminary order out of the Ephesian chaos.

1. Author

The traditional view is that the apostle Paul was the author of Ephesians. In the early church Paul was universally acknowledged to be the author of our document. He is mentioned in Eph. 1:1 and 3:1, and every early Christian who refers to the author names Paul. In addition, Ephesians is found in the earliest collections of the letters of Paul. For centuries Ephesians was understood by the church's scholars to be, with Philippians, Colossians, and Philemon, one of the prison epistles written by Paul during his first imprisonment in Rome.

More recently, however (actually starting already with Erasmus in the 16th century), serious objections to authorship by Paul have been raised by many students of the Pauline letters. These objections center around five significant areas: style, vocabulary, relationship of Ephesians to the rest of the NT, use made of the OT, and theology.

Style

The writing style of Ephesians is significantly different from the style of the undisputed letters of Paul.[2] Ephesians shows a preference for long, complex sentences. The author delights in piling up genitive constructions, relative clauses woven together and dependent on some far-distant verb, appositional phrases, and synonyms joined by the word "and." A good example is 1:15-23. The RSV is faithful to the Greek by printing that entire nine-verse sequence as the *one* sentence which it is in the Greek text.[3] A further example is the preceding section, 1:3-14, which the RSV divides into six sentences. Again, however, the Greek text shows only one sentence for that twelve-verse section.[4] Even the strong preference for indirect questions in Ephesians is untypical of the undisputed letters. Admittedly, evaluation of style is subjective, yet writing style is often such an unconscious thing that insights gained by study of an author's style can be of great help in determining the authenticity of a document.[5]

Vocabulary

There are significant differences in vocabulary between Ephesians and the undisputed letters. First, there are many words peculiar to Ephesians. More than 80 words that occur in Ephesians are *not* found elsewhere in Pauline material. Thirty-eight of them are found nowhere else in the entire NT (this phenomenon is not unusual: Romans and 1 and 2 Corinthians each have about 100 words found nowhere else in the NT). Second and more significant, Ephesians' peculiar vocabulary associates it not with Paul's letters but with later writings of the NT. Many unusual terms from the undisputed letters of Paul *are* found elsewhere only in the later writings of the NT and in the early fathers of the church. Among those terms are "freely bestowed" in 1:6, "beloved" as a reference to Christ in 1:6, "commonwealth" in 2:12, "likeness" in 4:24, and "debauchery" in 5:18.

Third, certain major Pauline words are either used strangely or omitted entirely. Thus while the Jew/Gentile issue is significant for Ephesians, the term *Jews* is never used; Paul, however, used it often. In addition, the all-important Pauline term *law* is missing in the relevant discussions in Ephesians. Instead of *Satan*, the word *devil* is employed. Of great import is that the word *justify* is not utilized to describe the activity of God. Moreover, in addition to the Pauline term *heavens (ouranoi)* we find the non-Pauline term *heavenly places (epouraniois)*. Also intriguing are the new meanings given in Ephesians to terms that *are* found in the undisputed letters. Such terms include *mystery, church, inheritance, fulness,* and *save;* other examples are *stewardship, possessions,* and *sum up.* In addition, the prepositions *in (en)* and *according to (kata)* are used far more often in Ephesians than in the undisputed letters.

Relationship of Ephesians to the Rest of the NT

For many scholars the apparent dependency of Ephesians on the rest of the NT is decisive in their evaluation of Ephesians as written by someone other than Paul. Especially intriguing is the relationship with Colossians. Approximately one-third of the words in Colossians are found also in Ephesians; to turn around the comparison: one-fourth of the words in Ephesians appear in Colossians. A simple explanation would be that both works are by the same author. There are two reasons, however, why such an approach is an inadequate explanation:

a. If both were by the same author, it is rather odd that words and phrases from different parts of Colossians appear together in new constructions in Ephesians. So, for example, Col. 2:11-14 and 1:21-22 are brought together in Eph. 2:11-15; Eph. 4:16 appears to be a combination of Col. 1:18; 2:2, 19.[6]

b. If both were by the same author, it is quite difficult to determine when they were written. Persons who argue for Pauline authorship of both must also argue that the letters were written within a very short span of time. Yet that theory founders on the rock of word usage, for a number of loaded terms are used differently in the two documents; such a shift in usage is difficult to explain if the two letters are from the same hand, writing during the same time period. The word *oikonomia*, e.g., which is translated in the RSV as "plan," "stewardship," and "office," is used differently in Ephesians and Colossians. In Ephesians the term refers to God's task as a strategy or planned economy (1:10; 3:2, 9); in Colossians it refers to Paul's task (1:25; Eph. 3:2 is an especially clear contrast with this verse). Other concepts that are used differently include *mystery* and *fulness*.

Distinct word usages argue against a common author. The high level of duplication of material, though, argues for a literary dependence. How is such a dependence to be explained? Or, to state it baldly, who used whom? It seems more likely that Ephesians is dependent on Colossians, that is, that the author of Ephesians used Colossians.[7] In Col. 4:7-9, for example, the author commends Tychicus to the Colossians and concludes in 4:10-18 with a series of personal greetings. In Ephesians the same commendation of Tychicus occurs almost verbatim in 6:21-22. What is quite odd, however, is that the commendation in Ephesians is not merely the only such greeting near the conclusion of the letter, it is the sole personal greeting in the entire document. To put it in other words, the Ephesian greeting suddenly springs up, with no preparation and with no supporting cast. A second sign of dependence on Colossians is found in Ephesians 5, which appears to be an expansion and further Christianization of material found already in Colossians 3. Thus Colossians has two verses on proper marital relationships (3:18-19); Ephesians has thirteen (5:21-33). Obviously, if Ephesians *is* dependent on Colossians, and Colossians is *not* written by Paul,[8] the likelihood that Paul wrote Ephesians is slim indeed.

Ephesians is also without question dependent on other letters of Paul. Thus Eph. 2:18 and 3:11-12 are based on Rom. 5:1-12, and Eph. 1:11 appears to be formulated from Rom. 8:28.[9] It is conceivable that Paul is simply quoting himself, but the probability of that explanation is considerably weakened when one discovers that there is no other letter attributed to Paul which exhibits anything like this kind or degree of "borrowing."

Further possible dependencies surface when one compares Ephesians with 1 Peter, Hebrews, Acts, and the Johannine literature, all documents from the later strata of the NT.[10] The situation with regard to Acts is especially instructive. It has long been acknowledged that Acts has no knowledge of the pillar epistles of Paul and only slightly more appreciation for the distinctive theology of Paul. It is therefore striking that ten of the unusual words found in Ephesians occur elsewhere in the NT only in Luke-Acts.

Use Made of the OT

Ephesians also uses OT material in ways significantly different from the undisputed letters of Paul.[11] While Paul usually introduces OT citations with a formula ("as it is written"; "he says"), only in Eph. 4:8 do we find a comparable introductory formula. The wording of that formula, however, is found only in Ephesians in the entire Pauline corpus ("therefore it is said," *dio legei*). Moreover, the same formula is used in 5:14 to introduce an early Christian hymn. Significant variation is also found in the *way* Scripture is used. Whereas in the Jew/Gentile discussions of Galatians 3–4 and Romans 4; 9–11; 15 the OT plays a key role, in Ephesians the OT is used only incidentally and indirectly when addressing the same issue (2:17). In addition, Ephesians does not use nearly so strongly the promise-fulfillment scheme of the Galatians and Romans material; indeed, such a scheme would be inappropriate, given the opinion expressed in Eph. 3:5 that the mystery of the inclusion of the Gentiles " . . . was not made known to the sons of men in other generations . . . ." Another distinction in usage is seen at Eph. 5:31, where Gen. 2:24 is quoted. The same OT passage is quoted in 1 Cor. 6:16, but it is used in a very different way. A third example leads into the next section, on theology. In Eph. 6:1 children are told to obey their parents. The OT basis is given in vv. 2 and 3. Not only is the promise of earthly reward unusual for Paul, but the whole perspective of promised long life is odd for an apostle who expected the imminent end of the world.

Theology

A final argument is determinative for many, namely, that the theology of Ephesians is so distinctive when viewed in relationship to the undisputed letters that it is not possible to conceive of Paul as the author.

Chief among the distinctive features is the lack of any expectation of the imminent end of the world. The end has been postponed to such an extent that it simply passes out of view. Paul's distinction between present-time justification and future salvation is lost; Ephesians speaks of salvation as a past experience (2:5, 8). Related is the fact that, as opposed to the pillar epistles, time categories are less significant than space categories. Thus in chap. 1 the resurrection and ascension of Christ are viewed spatially (1:20-22); in similar fashion the author writes of the effects of Christ on the believer (2:4-6). For that matter, even alienation from Christ can be expressed in spatial terms (2:12-13, 17-19). The church itself is seen in cosmic (that is, spatial) terms, since it is the means through which God reveals his wisdom ". . . to the principalities and powers in the heavenly places" (3:10). Also related to relaxation of end-time expectation is the fact that believers already in some way share in Christ's resurrection (2:5-6; contrast Rom. 6:4-5, where Paul is very careful not to intimate that Christians have already been resurrected); at the same time, it is intriguing to note that Ephesians has no reference to dying with Christ. Many wonder whether the lofty view of marriage outlined in 5:22-33 can be reconciled with 1 Corinthians 7, where Paul advises people not to marry. In 1 Cor. 3:11 Paul firmly states that the foundation of the church is Jesus Christ. In Eph. 2:20, however, the household of God is "built upon the foundation of the apostles and prophets, Christ Jesus himself being the cornerstone"; the exalted view of apostles is also indicated in Eph. 3:5. Instead of the continuing struggle for his apostleship which is fundamental in the pillar epistles, we find in Ephesians an almost romanticized view of apostleship. Also difficult to reconcile is the Ephesian understanding of the central mystery of the gospel, the joining of Jews and Gentiles in one body (3:3-6). Besides the fact that in 1 Corinthians Paul speaks of many "mysteries of God" (4:1), the Ephesian view of mystery is significantly different in that the perspective on the Jew/Gentile issue is totally reversed. In Romans and Galatians the issue is how Gentiles may be included in the (Jewish-) Christian Church. In Ephesians, on the other hand, the fear is that the Gentile-dominated church will lose its Jewish roots. Ephesians thus reflects a later stage of the discussion when the inclusion of Gentiles can be addressed in a somewhat traditionally Pauline, yet less polemical, way (2:1-22), since the issue appears to have been settled long since. Related is the judgment of Ephesians that the law is simply abolished (2:14-15). This outright antinomianism is contrary to the historical Paul (see Rom. 3:31).

The church of the author of Ephesians, moreover, thinks of itself not as a group on the brink of the end but as an institution with a future in the world. Concern for that future is seen in the heightened interest in the way Christians are to live in this world which is not passing away. The household duties in 5:21—6:9 are evidence of a growing concern for life in this world; there is nothing comparable in the undisputed letters. Even the concept of *church* is affected. In the undisputed letters the church (*ek-klēsia*) is the house church; only in 1 Cor. 15:9 and Phil. 3:6 does Paul refer to the church in general, when he speaks of persecuting the church. In Ephesians, though, the *ekklēsia* is the universal church; it is a cosmic entity that unites all Christians on earth and in the heavenly places. Some scholars (particularly Ernst Käsemann) have argued that in Ephesians emphasis is diverted from the work of Christ to the work of the church to such an extent that Ephesians can be called "early catholic."[12]

Another major theological distinction concerns the figure of Christ. In Eph. 1:22-23 and 4:15-16 (as in Col. 1:18 and 2:19) Christ is the head of his body, the church. In 1 Corinthians 12 and Romans 12, however, Christ is not the head of the body, even though the church is called the body of Christ. The difference may seem minor, but in 1 Corinthians and Romans Paul utilizes the body analogy from Greek political thought; the Ephesian concept, however, is more dependent on a mythical—and perhaps Gnostic—concept. In general, Christ is viewed more from a cosmic perspective in Ephesians than in the undisputed letters.

Conclusion

When discussing the authorship of Ephesians we move in the area of probability. Is it a *fact* that Paul wrote Ephesians? Not even the most ardent defender of apostolic authorship could claim that. Is it *possible* that Paul wrote Ephesians? Of course it is—but is it *probable*? To the thesis of non-Pauline authorship suggested in this commentary one could raise serious objections. Ephesians, for example, utilizes a great deal of traditional material, much of it hymnic-liturgical. Could not that material have affected the style of Paul's writing? Of course it could have, but one would still need to explain the fact that such a phenomenon does not occur to such an extent in any of the undisputed writings. Why could Paul not vary in the ways in which he used a given term? Could not his vocabulary as well as his theology develop in new directions over the years? Of course they could, but the question of probability remains: is it probable that Paul's thought would change so radically in so short a period of time? Determination of an author for Ephesians is an exercise in probability, and the final question is whether it is probable that in one brief work Paul would exhibit such strong peculiarities in such major areas as style, vocabulary, relationship to his other writings, use of the OT, and theology. Or is it more probable that someone other than Paul wrote this work?

Who then wrote Ephesians? The most that can be said is that Ephesians was written by a follower of Paul who, while quite likely himself a Jew (2:3, 11, 17) was profoundly influenced not only by ideas from Qumran but also from Hellenism in general and Gnosticism in particular. The author was himself a creative thinker who sought to apply Paul's insights in a new situation. The author also used Paul's name. To modern sensitivities such pseudonymity (writing in the name of another person) seems awkward and indeed rather dishonest. We think in terms of copyright laws and authorship in a strict sense. The ancient world simply did not operate that way. During the NT era the writing of pseudonymous letters was common both in Judaism and in Christianity (Letter of Jeremiah, Letter of Aristeas, 1 and 2 Peter, Jude, Pastoral Epistles, James, Revelation, Acts 23:26-30, 2 Clement, Barnabas). Apparently a Christian author would write in the name of an apostle in order to gain readier acceptance for a new piece of literature and also to say what the apostle would have said in a new situation.[13] Pseudonymity was not "bad" or deceitful but was an accepted practice of the day. Nor should pseudonymity be seen as lessening the value of the writing. Rather, what we have in the pseudonymous work called Ephesians is an updated reapplication of Pauline theology to a new day.

2. Destination

The traditional view of the destination of Ephesians is quite simple: it was written to Christians in Ephesus and hence was designated with the superscription "To the Ephesians." In addition there is the clear reference in Eph. 1:1: "To the saints who are at Ephesus and faithful in Christ Jesus" (RSV footnote).

Both traditional points are weak. The superscription was not part of the original document. Titles were added when several letters were recopied together onto one scroll or codex. That process may have begun in the 90s of the first century, although definite proof for the superscription is found only in the latter part of the second century. One second-century figure, Marcion, thought that what we call "Ephesians" was in fact a letter written to the Laodiceans. No other manuscript evidence supports Marcion, but the mere existence of his option indicates the relative fluidity of the situation.

But what of the place-name in 1:1? Manuscript evidence is divided. The reading "at" or "in Ephesus" is found in the fifth-century manuscript, Alexandrinus, as well as in the second correctors of Sinaiticus and Vaticanus. The words are omitted, however, in the original copies of the two great fourth-century manuscripts, Sinaiticus and Vaticanus, as well as by the earliest manuscript of Ephesians, p[46] (ca. A.D. 200). Nor are the words found in many early church writers. Apparently the superscription, which was becoming fixed by the end of the second century, gave birth by the beginning of the fifth century to the words "at Ephesus." The RSV, in recognition of the weight of the manuscript evidence, reads: "To the saints who are also faithful in Christ Jesus."

The omission of the words "at Ephesus" creates an awkward Greek construction, however; in part to answer that difficulty various scholars have developed the theory that in the original document a blank spot was left. Since the "letter" was meant to be encyclical, the reader in a given city could read his or her city's name when reading the letter at worship, thus localizing the salutation. This theory, ingenious as it is, fails on three counts: (1) if the theory were valid, only the place-name would have been changed; all the manuscripts which omit Ephesus, however, also omit "at" or "in"; (2) there are no ancient parallels to this practice; and (3) it is extremely odd, if the theory is valid, that we have no manuscripts with place-names other than Ephesus.

That our document was not addressed to Ephesus is substantiated by the relationship indicated between the author and the document's recipients. The Paul of Acts spent three years in Ephesus establishing a congregation (Acts: 18:19-21; 19:1-20; 20:17-38). In Ephesians, however, the author and the recipients do not know each other (1:15; 3:2-3; 4:21); he has only hearsay knowledge about them. Nor for that matter do we have the sort of direct discussion of specific situations that we find in the undisputed letters. The impression is of a more general work not nearly so tied to particular problems of a particular congregation. Even personal greetings are absent. When we recall the manuscript problems, we must conclude that Ephesus was not the original destination of "Ephesians."

What was? At most we can say that it is probable, given the dependence on Colossians and in particular the reference to Tychicus, that the letter was addressed to Christians in Asia Minor. The addressees were also primarily Gentile Christians (chap. 2).

3. Purpose and Genre

In the previous section we touched briefly on the theory that Ephesians was written as a circular or encyclical letter. A prominent alternative to that view is the theory of E. J. Goodspeed.[14] He argued that Paul's letters, since they were written for highly specific purposes, were soon forgotten. But near the end of the first century a Christian in Colossae read about Paul in Acts and was inspired to gather the Pauline letters. To update them he wrote an introduction in order to summarize Paul's understanding of the faith. He used Colossians as his basic source, but he also used letters he had collected, as well as the book of Acts. The name of the introductory letter? Ephesians. Who was this anonymous Colossian writer? Why, the slave Onesimus, who is the topic of the letter to Philemon. The Onesimus of Philemon, argued Goodspeed, was the same Onesimus who was bishop of Ephesus early in the second century. While the Onesimus part of the theory is accepted by almost no one, the theory that Ephesians was an introductory letter has remained popular since Goodspeed introduced it. Its popularity is unfortunate, for the theory falters at three points: (1) there is no proof that Paul was so completely forgotten and that only Acts saved him from obscurity; (2) we have no manuscript in which Ephesians is the first of the Pauline letters; (3) the content of Ephesians cannot be explained by this theory.

A second theory based in part on Goodspeed, but which moves in a new direction, is that of John C. Kirby.[15] Once more, a collection of Paul's letters sparked the production of Ephesians. An elder of the church in Ephesus was asked to furnish the collector of Paul's letters with a copy of his correspondence to Ephesus. Since no correspondence existed he wrote our Ephesians on the basis of his memory of Paul's preaching. In addition he structured the work around the Pentecost liturgy followed by the early church; included in that service was the Baptism of new believers. While the reason he gives for the composition of Ephesians is unsupported by anything other than his own theories and while the assignment of Ephesians to a specific liturgy is more exact than the sources permit, Kirby's work does highlight two important areas we will discuss again: (1) the document's liturgical language, and (2) its connection with Baptism.

A third theory points to a different author. Ralph P. Martin identifies, as we have already done, parallels in language and theology between Acts and Ephesians. On that basis he hypothesizes a common author for the two documents—Luke.[16] The Lukan connection does not seem substantial enough to support the sort of relationship Martin posits; moreover, Luke as author of Ephesians depends on Luke the physician, traveling companion of Paul, as the author of Acts. The latter basis is thin indeed.

While Ephesians is not nearly so obvious in revealing its purpose and situation as is Galatians, for example, it is possible to put together into a coherent whole the various threads that have been delineated. Nils Dahl in his various writings to a large degree has done that pulling together.[17] The recipients had been pagans and now they are Christians. It is also clear from the document that Paul had not been the missionary who had converted them. We are thereby, according to Dahl, given the reasons for the writing of Ephesians:

a. To establish a relationship between Paul and the recipients. In his earlier writings Dahl meant the historical Paul. More recently he looks rather to the need to mediate the apostle's presence to Gentile Christians separated from him in time rather than space;[18] that is, the author wants his work to be the means whereby the now-dead Paul can become, in a sense, a living apostle for the author's time.

b. To remind the recipients of their blessings and to recall their responsibilities as believers. Dahl sees Ephesians as a letter of congratulations to these believing Gentiles, as well as a reminder of the ethical implications of their beliefs. The focus of the remembering is Baptism (1:3-14; 2:6, 19-22; 4:4-5, for example). Building on Dahl, we can identify an indicative-imperative scheme in Ephesians that is fundamental to its structure. That is, the author first reminds his readers of what God has done for them and only then does he call for the response. The history of God's activity with the recipients is the basis of their action. That does not mean, however, that all instruction is confined to chaps. 4–6; it is found already in chaps. 1–3.

c. To overcome separation between Gentile believers and their Jewish predecessors and contemporaries. The recipients are in danger of forfeiting the church's rootage in and identification with not only Jewish Christianity but with Judaism itself. Besides the sheer content of the work itself, the repeated use of the OT serves as a corrective to any beginning Marcionite tendency.

In all of this the author employs language and categories that are not only familiar to his people but which are drawn from their catechetical and liturgical life. The exhortations in chaps. 4–6 are particularly associated with the catechetical process of the early church, and hymns and other liturgical language are repeatedly quoted (1:3-14, 20-23; 2:14-18, for example) as the author seeks to establish those positive linkages which are so important for any communication—and as he seeks to remind them of their heritage. Thus Ephesians is properly to be categorized as a baptismal reminder and exhortation, and not as a theological meditation or tractate. The epistolary structure, in addition, is merely an outer framework for the construction of the author's thoughts. Missing are a specific address (see earlier comments on 1:1), any mention of travel plans (which makes the secondary nature of 6:21-22 that much more significant), and the normal Pauline greetings at the end of the letter. Ephesians is also the only letter assigned to Paul which has both a eulogy (1:3-14) and a thanksgiving (1:15-23) at the beginning of the letter.

While Dahl has been most insightful, he has been less helpful thus far in relating Ephesians to the literary categories of the first century. One type of oral and written literature that may provide insight into the genre of Ephesians is the category of ancient rhetoric called epideictic.[19] Originally epideictic speech was a speech given simply to display the rhetorical talents of the speech giver (*epideiksis* means "showing forth," "display"). Soon, however, the epideictic speech came to focus on a present-time situation that called for praise and/or blame. In carrying out the task the epideictic orator engaged in much amplification; in addition he gave a great deal of attention to good character (cf. the writing style and content of Ephesians). Epideictic style and concerns were transferred to prose literature, including epistles. While epideictic literature could address many issues, it usually was devoted to praising a person, object, or event. One subcategory was the congratulatory speech (written or oral).[20] The congratulatory speech, as well as the other categories of epideictic literature, often narrated the past events for which praise was being given (cf. Ephesians 2), using the praise as the basis for paraenesis (exhortation; cf. Ephesians 4–6). The epilog, or concluding section, was to be full of emotion, as the author sought not only to summarize the argument but also to make a final appeal to the heart (cf. Eph. 6:10-20). Thus Ephesians, written by an author who needs to introduce himself, builds on the commonalities of religious experience, language, and liturgy in order to establish a sense of communion between author and audience. Moreover, the educational purpose of epideictic literature is seen clearly in both the overall tone of the work and in the more clearly catechetical material. Our outline of Ephesians has been constructed with this framework in mind.

The discussion of genre fits in well with the purpose we have listed for Ephesians. The author congratulates the Gentile recipients on their inclusion in the Christian church and spurs them on to live out fully the implications of that inclusion. In developing his thoughts the author touches base with two intriguing and complex movements of antiquity, Qumran (the community of the Dead Sea Scrolls) and Gnosticism.

The Dead Sea Scrolls are the literary deposit of a Jewish apocalyptic movement that flourished during the two centuries before Christ as well as during the first two-thirds of the first century A.D. Concepts from Ephesians that seem related to the Scrolls include "election," "predestination," "mystery," conflicting spirits of light and darkness, spiritual warfare, exhortations, the community as a holy house or temple, and the revealing of the divine plan of salvation. The Greek of Ephesians exhibits strong Semitic coloring which is especially parallel to the Hebrew of the Dead Sea Scrolls, most especially to the style of the hymns. Was the author of Ephesians directly dependent on the Dead Sea Scrolls? Probably not. More likely he and the writers of the Scrolls utilized the same style of Jewish liturgical writing, which in turn has its roots in the OT, the Christian connections with which the author of Ephesians was concerned to affirm.

The relationship with Gnosticism is much more disputed. Gnosticism was a wide-ranging movement that emphasized dualism, especially the contrast between spirit and matter; creation of the world by a demiurge, a sort of second-rate deity; entrapment of the divine spark in the outer physical body and hence the desire to escape this evil world; and spiritual knowledge, that flash of insight and comprehension that one's origin was not in this world but in the divine. Ephesians has at times been studied solely from the perspective of Gnosticism. While that position is extreme, there are concepts in Ephesians that have a distinctive Gnostic ring: "fulness"; "aeon"; "dividing wall"; "heavenlies"; descent and ascent of the redeemer figure who is the new man, perfect man, and head of the body, and who pacifies the "all" under his lordship; marriage as the image of the heavenly syzygy between Christ and the church (a "syzygy" is a pair of opposites, usually one of which is male and the other female); "knowledge"; and present-tense resurrection. There are also opponents mentioned in Ephesians (5:6-14), who may well exhibit Gnostic characteristics such as a disdain of marriage (cf. 5:21-33). Even the emphasis on the OT may in part be developed in response to the Gnostic view of the Hebrew God of the OT as the demiurge (intermediary shaper of the material world). That Gnostic influences were impacting on the churches of Asia Minor in the second half of the first century is clear in Colossians, 1 and 2 Timothy, Titus, and Revelation. That Ephesians was written in part to combat Gnostic influences seems probable.[21]

Ephesians, in sum, was a congratulatory communication written in letter format to Gentile Christians in Asia Minor. The Jewish-Christian author wrote in the name of Paul in order to establish a relationship between the apostle to the Gentiles and his spiritual heirs. In reminding them of their blessings he also reminded them of their responsibilities, especially in light of the growing separation experienced between Gentile Christians and Jewish Christians and Jews in general and in light of Gnostic threats. Ephesians is thus a dramatic call for unity based on God's activity, especially as centered in Baptism. It also functions as a summary of Paul's theology, but a summary for a new day and time.

And what is that day and time? It is after the lifetime of Paul and after the apostolic age in general (see 2:20). The apostles, including Paul, are viewed from a distance, and the battle of Paul's ministry for the inclusion of Gentiles into a Jewish-dominated church has become a struggle to retain the Jewish connection in an essentially Gentile church. The fact that Ephesians may be used by other Christian writers as early as A.D. 95 (1 Clement), and certainly by 117 (Ignatius of Antioch), would suggest that Ephesians must have been written by at least 90. In fact, the dates usually assigned are 80–100. The dates of 75–90 give us a span beginning about a decade after Paul's death and extending to a point approximately five years before Ephesians was used by others and five years before the first collecting of Pauline material may well have occurred, a collecting that included Ephesians. Obviously all dating is approximate, but the postapostolic age is a firm placement.

OUTLINE OF EPHESIANS

The genre of Ephesians has already been identified as that of epideictic speech structured according to an epistolary format. The first half of the letter (chaps. 1–3) reminds Christians of who they were and who now, by God's action, they are. While already in the initial three chapters ethical implications are drawn it is especially in chaps. 4–6 that those implications are developed. Ephesians ends its appeal with a strong emotional statement about the warfare of the Christian (6:10-20) and a standard epistolary conclusion (6:21-24).

I. Salutation (1:1-2)
   A. Name and Title of Sender (1:1a)
   B. Recipients (1:1b)
   C. Greeting (1:2)
II. Blessing of God (1:3-14)
   A. Identification of the One Blessed (1:3-6)
   B. Further Identification of God's Relationship to "Us": We Have Been Redeemed (1:7-10)
   C. Further Identification of God's Relationship to "Us": We Have Been Destined (1:11-12)
   D. Further Identification of God's Relationship to "You": You Were Sealed (1:13-14)
III. Thanksgiving (1:15-23)
   A. Reason for Thanksgiving (1:15)
   B. Thanksgiving Proper (1:16-23)

IV. Narration: God's Love (2:1-10)
    A. Statement of the Gentiles' Condition (2:1-2)
    B. Statement of the Jews' Condition and of the Condition of All (2:3*ab*)
    C. Result (2:3*c*)
    D. The Divine "But" (2:4-10)
 V. Admonition to Remember (2:11-22)
    A. Negative Remembrance (2:11-12)
    B. Positive Remembrance (2:13)
    C. Hymn of Praise to Christ (2:14-18)
    D. Ecclesiastical Implications (2:19-22)
 VI. Prayer of the Apostle (3:1-21)
    A. Identification of the Suppliant (3:1)
    B. Digression on Paul's Credentials and His Gospel (3:2-13)
       1. Description of the Message Assumed Heard (3:2-6)
       2. Paul's Credentials (3:7-13)
    C. Prayer Resumed (3:14-21)
VII. Exhortation/Paraenesis (4:1—6:20)
    A. Introduction (4:1*a*)
    B. Basic Exhortation (4:1*b*-6)
    C. Elaboration on Unity in Terms of Gifts (4:7-16)
    D. Return to Basic Exhortation (4:17—6:20)
       1. Negative Exhortation (4:17-19)
       2. Positive Exhortation Based on Baptism (4:20-24)
       3. Implications (4:25—5:2)
          a. Exhortation One: Truthfulness (4:25)
          b. Exhortation Two: Sinless Anger (4:26-27)
          c. Exhortation Three: Stealing (4:28)
          d. Exhortation Four: Speech (4:29)
          e. Exhortation Five: the Spirit (4:30)
          f. Exhortation Six: Behavior in the Community (4:31-32)
          g. Exhortation Seven: Summary (5:1-2)
       4. Exhortations on Negative Behavior (5:3-20)

Ephesians

COMMENTARY

■ Salutation (1:1-2)

Ephesians opens with a rather typical Jewish-Christian salutation. Whereas the normal Greek epistolary salutation was quite brief (sender to recipients, greetings; see James 1:1), the Jewish salutation was expanded to include attributes of both author and reader, as well as a blessing. Yet while the Ephesian salutation is more extensive than Greek salutations, it is quite modest and succinct when compared to the more elaborate constructions in Rom. 1:1-7; 1 Cor. 1:1-3; and Gal. 1:1-5.

Name and Title of Sender (1:1a)

The pseudonymous author uses Paul's Roman name; it is of more than casual interest that only Paul is named, since in Colossians Timothy is included as a cosender. The special function of Paul as apostle in this letter requires, in a sense, that Paul be the only sender, for he is the one to whom the mystery of God's activity has been made known (3:3, 7-9; cf. Gal. 1:15-16; 1 Cor. 9:1). He is immediately designated as **an apostle of Christ Jesus by the will of God. Apostle** is at one and the same time his title, his function, and his directive. The terms **Paul, an apostle** go together much as do Jesus Christ; in both, a personal name and title become unified. Apostle means "one who is sent," "a representative," even "an ambassador" (see 6:20 where the author says, "I am an ambassador [*presbeuō*] in chains"). Paul constantly had to struggle for the right to use this title and so it appears as his self-designation at the beginnings of Romans, 1 and 2 Corinthians, Galatians, and Colossians. Paul, as a representative, does not stand on his own, though; he represents Christ Jesus, indeed he carries as Christ's apostle the authority of Christ himself. He is sent by and "commissioned" (NEB) by Christ. Nor did Paul simply aspire to be an apostle. His apostleship is the result of the very **will of God.** The term "will" appears again in vv. 5, 9, and 11 of our present chapter and is used also in 5:17 and 6:6 with reference to Lord and God. It, together with "purpose," "choose," and "destine," indicates that in Ephesians there is a strong sense of the activity and direction of God.

Recipients (1:1*b*)

The basic designation of the recipients is that they are **saints.**[1] The term does not, however, carry the moral connotations it has garnered in contemporary language ("she is a real saint"). The Greek word for "saint" also means "holy"; the related verb is "to sanctify." One is "holy" in the Bible not by being morally perfect, but by being in a positive relationship with the Holy One, God (of people, Exod. 19:6; Lev. 11:44-45; of places, Exod. 29:31; Lev. 6:16; of times, Exod. 31:14; Lev. 23:8). The term is an honorific title for Israel in both the OT and in the Dead Sea Scrolls. By using it the author applies to the new covenant people the language and theology of the old covenant and makes "saints" a term for all Christians (1:15; 3:8, 18; 4:12; 5:3; 6:18). At the same time the author reminds the recipients of their rootage in Judaism. The readers are **saints** as those **who are also faithful in Christ Jesus. Faithful** belongs to the same word family as "faith" and "believe," a pair of words that occur repeatedly in the letter (1:13, 15, 19; 2:8; 3:12, 17; 4:5, 13; 6:16, 23). Saints, therefore, have a positive relationship with God not by virtue of descent but of faith. And it is a faith whose center is in Messiah Jesus, into whom believers are incorporated at Baptism.[2]

Greeting (1:2)

As elsewhere in Pauline letters the standard Jewish greeting (**peace**) is combined with a modified form of the Greek greeting (**grace**). This formula ought not, however, to be passed by too quickly. **Grace** is the unmerited love of God by which God saves (2:5,8). The term is prominent throughout the letter, occurring in every chapter except the fifth; in addition to its connections with the Greek epistolary greeting, **grace** is used in the Greek OT to translate the Hebrew *hēn*, which refers to God's unilateral activity for humanity. **Peace** (the Hebrew *shalôm*) refers to everything that makes life worth living; it too is used repeatedly in Ephesians, especially in 2:14-17, and it is a Pauline shorthand word for the blessings of salvation (Rom. 5:1; Phil. 4:7). The terms occur in close proximity once again in 6:23-24, although in reverse order. Thus the letter is bracketed by the terms of greeting. It is, finally, of great significance to note the source of the greeting: **from God our Father and the Lord Jesus Christ.** Both noun complexes are governed by the one preposition **from**; in Greek this construction indicates a unity of action (see also 1:3,6,17). God acts through Christ, and the centrality of Christology in Ephesians is indicated already by the three occurrences of **Christ** in our first two verses.

■ Blessing of God (1:3-14)

As in 2 Cor. 1:3-4 and 1 Peter 1:3-12, the salutation is followed by a section that blesses God for his gifts.[3] This kind of material was common in Jewish documents of antiquity and was called the *berakah;* the ancient form has been recovered in contemporary Eucharistic prayers ("Blessed are you, Lord of heaven and earth"; *LBW*, p. 33). The blessing (which can also be called a benediction or eulogy), since it was written in the language of praise, was a natural location for the use of hymnic material. In fact, scholars have frequently identified in this blessing an underlying hymn, which has been variously analyzed. One analysis identifies a hymn with the two stanzas of vv. 5-8 and 9-12a; other analyses add vv. 3-4 as an opening stanza. A more detailed study suggests that v. 3 is the introduction; vv. 4-6 are a general treatment of the theme, with vv. 7-8, 9-10, and 11-12 being more refined expositions; and vv. 13-14 are a concluding stanza applying the hymn to the addressees. Attempts have been made to analyze the passage by means of recurring phrases such as **the praise of his glory** (vv. 6, 12, 14) or **in Christ/in him** (many times throughout the passage). Certainly our verses have hymnic features: liturgical language, frequent participial constructions, and multiple relative clauses. On the other hand, it is difficult to sustain the argument that we have here an actual *quoted* hymn, since there is no identifiable distinction between the style of this particular section and the style of the rest of the document. If there is an actual hymn here it has been so carefully integrated, or its style is so close to that of the letter's author, that we can no longer identify an underlying, pre-Ephesian hymn—if indeed there ever was one. Perhaps that is just the point: the author of Ephesians can use liturgical language and a hymnic style even in passages that no one would call actual hymns. The style of Ephesians is, in fact, quite close to the style of many of the hymns in the Dead Sea Scrolls. At the most, we can say that in 1:3-14 there are hymnic elements.[4]

Of great importance is the twofold function of the blessing section. Certainly it blesses God for what God has done, but we need to recall that the blessing is written to be read and heard by the very people whom God has thus blessed. That is to say, one of the functions of the blessing is to remind the readers of what God has done for them. The reminder also serves as a subtle but substantive congratulations to the recipients for having been thus blessed. One function of the blessing, then, is that of reminder and congratulations, a function we have already identified as a major purpose of Ephesians (cf. Aristotle, *Ars Rhetorica* 3.14.1-11). The author also establishes contact with his readers by identifying himself with them (**our, us**). The second function of the blessing is to state the major themes to be developed in the rest of the letter: **in Christ,** "the heavenlies," **mystery, grace, purpose, fulness, Spirit.** The Jew/Gentile problem is reflected in vv. 13-14 and perhaps v. 11. It is quite significant, too, that thoughts introduced in the blessing become the basis for ethical action in the paraenesis: chosen to be holy and blameless, adopted by God, and sealed by the Spirit—all these will surface in our later discussions.

Identification of the One Blessed (1:3-6)

The very first word, **blessed,** is the marker that identifies the section. But who is the one who is blessed? He is **the God and Father of our Lord Jesus Christ;** that is, the "blessed one" is first of all identified by means of his relationship with Christ. That relationship determines the rest of the blessing, where we find **in Christ, in him,** or **through him** occurring about a dozen times. While God (as Father) is seen as distinct from and, we may probably say, superior to Jesus Christ, it is in and through Christ that God acts. God's activity is designated by three verbs (all aorist participles in Greek): he **has blessed us in Christ** (v. 3); **he chose us in him** (v. 4); and **he destined us . . . through Jesus Christ** (v. 5). In each case the activity for which the author blesses God is a completed action that cannot be revoked. God has acted, and the results are sure.

In v. 3 one notices the rhetorical device of using several forms of the same word family: *blessed* **be the God . . . who has** *blessed* **us in Christ with every spiritual** *blessing* **in the heavenly places.**[5] The blessing may well be that given to Abraham, a blessing that includes all nations (chap. 2; Gal. 3:6-14; Gen. 12:2-3; 22:17). **The heavenly places,** already noted in the Introduction as a term peculiar to Ephesians, refers to the divine realm. Blessings kept there cannot be harmed. The inviolability of the blessings is shown not only by their location but also by the way in which God has brought them about: **in Christ,** a phrase which, when **in him** is included, occurs between 30 and 35 times in Ephesians.

In the pillar epistles "in Christ" refers to the intensely individual relationship of the believer who by Baptism is made part of the body of Christ. While that sense may underlie the usage of Ephesians, much stronger is the instrumental use; that is, "in Christ" chiefly expresses *how* God acts. The activity of God in blessing is further detailed by **chose** and **destined.** The verb **chose** is literally the word "elect"; the word **destined** is the Greek word for "foresaw." The electing activity of God is no latebreaking development. It occurred before the world was created and it occurred **in him,** that is, in Christ. Likewise, in his love, God foresaw (**destined**) through Jesus Christ that the recipients would be God's children.

As in the salutation, the author here in the blessing applies OT imagery to Christians. God chose Israel, not because they were numerous (Deut. 7:7) nor because they were more righteous than others (Deut. 9:4-6), but because God loved them (Deut. 23:5). And God made Israel his child (e.g., Exod. 4:22; Jer. 31:20). What we have, then, is predestination. We need to remember that the context is that of a blessing. More specifically, the passage is an ascription of praise to God for what he has done for Christians. There is not a word here about those who are *not* Christians, and there is here no doctrine of "double predestination" of both saved and damned. The message, in fact, is one that is tremendously positive: God chooses us, we do not choose God. And God's choice is not some cavalier, spur-of-the-moment decision which can be as easily changed; God's choice of us is prior to the creation of the world. No wonder Luther called predestination the doctrine of comfort (see also Rom. 8:28-30; 1 Peter 1:2, 20). So the Christian naturally wants to be **holy and blameless** (see the same words in 5:27) and to praise God's **glorious grace.** And the Christian can so be and do, by means of the adoption at Baptism (see Gal. 3:26-27). All of this happens, as if we could forget, **in the Beloved.** A similar expression is used for Jesus in the baptism accounts (Mark 1:11 and parallels) and in the transfiguration accounts (Mark 9:7 and parallels).

Further Identification of God's Relationship to "Us": We Have Been Redeemed (1:7-10)

Each of the next three sections begins with the words **in him** (vv. 7, 11, 13). Each section details more fully how God in Christ has blessed the letter's recipients. **We have redemption.** The author uses the present tense to emphasize the reality of redemption, a term whose background is found especially in slavery for the payment of a fee to release a slave (see also Eph. 1:14; 4:30; Rom. 3:24; 8:23; 1 Cor. 1:30; Col. 1:14; Heb. 9:15; 11:35). Similar language is used for God, who redeems Israel (Exod. 6:6; 15:13; Deut. 7:8; 13:5; e.g.) and the same image is applied to Jesus (Mark 10:45; 1 Peter 1:18-19). So TEV translates: "For by the death of Christ we are set free." The redemption is specifically **through his blood,** which refers to the cross of Christ. Just as redemption of old was through the blood of the Passover lamb, so is the new act of redemption effected through blood. The redemption is further specified by the words, **the forgiveness of our trespasses.** Interestingly, the Greek term used here for **forgiveness** (*aphesis*) does not occur in any of the undisputed letters; in the entire Pauline corpus it occurs only here and in Col. 1:14. The term means "a sending away"; it was used of prisoners when they were released in court from their penalties. In Ephesians the sending away is connected with the death of Christ and happens **according to the riches of his grace which he lavished upon us.** The riches of God's activity are indicated also in 1:18; 2:7; 3:8, 16.

In Greek the words printed in the RSV in v. 9, **in all wisdom and insight,** are printed as part of v. 8; there is not much difference in meaning, whichever way the words are read. **Wisdom and insight** are part of the gifts of God; they refer in particular to a grasping of God's will, as v. 9 makes clear. Two points need to be emphasized. First, it is God alone who makes known his will; trances, rites, and magical incantations do not give the insight. Second, God's will is a **mystery,** although the word does not mean "mystery" as in a mystery novel or detective story. Rather, **mystery** is the counsel of God, the purpose and plan of

God previously hidden but now revealed. Thus the mystery is a mystery only to the outsider.

What is the mystery? It has three aspects. First, the mystery is intimately connected with Christ; it is **set forth in Christ** ("in him" in Greek). Second, the mystery revealed is **a plan for the fulness of time.** The Greek word for plan is *oikonomia*, the law of the household, from which the word "economy" derives. The mystery is God's economy or **plan for the fulness of time.** The latter phrase implies a succession of world periods (**time** is plural in Greek), with the Christians living in the last time. Third, the mystery is God's plan **to unite all things** in Christ. The word **unite** means to "sum up," and it is used for adding a column of figures. The sum was written at the top of the column instead of the bottom; the term means literally to "bring to a head." Buried, in fact, in this verb is the Greek word *head*, which in Ephesians is applied to Christ. He is the head in whom all things are brought to a head. And that unity is cosmic, including **things in heaven and things on earth** (see also Eph. 1:22-23 and Col. 1:15-20). There may well be a statement here against Gnosticism, which sharply divides heaven and earth. Frequent parallels have also been drawn to the term *mysteries* as used in the Dead Sea Scrolls, and the Hebrew concept (*raz*) has been understood as determinative for Ephesians. It is to be noted, however, that in Ephesians the concept of mystery is much more focused than it is at Qumran (the Dead Sea community); Ephesians knows only the singular form, not the plural, as in the Scrolls; in Ephesians the mystery is always connected with Christ, and, as we shall see in chap. 2, the mystery also means the inclusion of the Gentiles.

Further Identification of God's Relationship to "Us": We Have Been Destined (1:11-12)

The author picks up in v. 11 the theme of predestination which has already been mentioned in v. 5; v. 12, likewise, restates v. 6. The repetition appears to be the result of a shifting of gears. In vv. 3-10 the author has included himself as part of the "us." In vv. 11-12, though, he speaks of Jewish Christians in the first person plural. It is they **who first hoped in Christ.** In contrast is the **you** of v. 13, which refers to the Gentile-Christian recipients. Once more, there is extreme emphasis on God's intentional choice; note the terms **purpose, accomplishes, counsel,** and **will,** which are piled up in a typically Ephesian fashion.

Further Identification of God's Relationship to "You": You Were Sealed (1:13-14)

The concluding section of the blessing begins with the words that have become virtually a refrain: **in him.** A major shift in addressee occurs, though. The **we** of the preceding verses becomes the **you** of vv. 13ff. The author now turns specifically to address his readers. They have been involved in two chief activities: they have **heard** and they have been **sealed.** The essentially passive nature of the first verb and the clearly passive nature of the second emphasize God as the implied actor (cf. 2:8). What the Ephesians have heard is **the word of truth,** which is immediately further identified as **the gospel of your salvation.** The gospel (the good news of God's activity in Jesus Christ) is that word, that message, which expresses the saving truth. No other message can do that, for no other message has had revealed in it the mystery of God's plan (vv. 9-10). The Ephesians, for their part, **have believed in him** (the Greek is ambiguous and could refer to the gospel), and God **sealed** them (the divine passive construction implies God as the actor.) To seal meant to mark an object or person with a seal as a sign of ownership; the term is especially prominent in Revelation 7. The sealing was part of Christian Baptism and indicated that the baptized person belonged to God (cf. TEV: "God put his stamp of ownership on you"). The person is **sealed with** or by **the Holy Spirit.** And it is **the promised Spirit**—promised, that is, to Israel (2:12; 3:6; 6:2) but now given to Gentiles.

Once again, in Pauline theology the Spirit is normatively, although not exclusively, given at Baptism. We begin to come full circle. In Baptism the individual's status is changed. She or he becomes a child of God (v. 5). And what does the adopted child

receive? The **inheritance** (v. 14; see also Gal. 3:26-29). When
Gal. 3:26-29 is read in conjunction with our passage it becomes
quite clear that we are here dealing with Baptism. As in 2 Cor.
1:22 (a close parallel to our passage) and 5:5, the business term
guarantee or "down payment" is used of the Spirit. The presence
of the Spirit is the believer's assurance that God will bring his
plan to fulfillment (see also 4:30), the result of which is the praise
of God's glory. Thus the author begins his letter by recalling his
readers to their Baptism. At the same time he introduces the
mystery of God's wondrous inclusion of the Gentiles. The blessing
emphasizes the eternal plan of God established before the world
itself was created; the blessing further identifies the present results of that plan, even while looking forward to the plan's future
fulfillment. God acts above all in Christ, but the passage contains
the raw data for what later became the classic doctrine of the
Trinity, as we see the work of Father, Son, and Spirit.

◼ Thanksgiving (1:15-23)

The author in v. 15 moves into the section that is normally
expected at the beginning of a Pauline letter, the thanksgiving
(see the sections that begin at Rom. 1:8; 1 Cor. 1:4; Phil. 1:3;
Col. 1:3; 1 Thess. 1:2; 2 Thess. 1:3; Philemon 4). The thanksgiving
section is similar in function to the blessing (it is only Ephesians
that has both): it courts the readers by speaking positively of them
and it indicates areas in which the recipients need to progress
(for a similar phenomenon see the thanksgiving sections of Philippians, Philemon, and Colossians). He praises them for their
faith and love, but at the same time he also lets them know that
they need to gain greater insight and a livelier hope. In so addressing his recipients he builds on themes already stated in 1:3-
14, as will be discussed below.

Reason for Thanksgiving (1:15)

The thanksgiving is loosely linked to the preceding section by the words **for this reason.** The link without question refers to vv. 13-14, which specifically address the Gentile recipients, but it likely also refers to the entire blessing and its rehearsal of God's benefits. The author gives two reasons for his thanksgiving for the recipients: their **faith in the Lord Jesus** (a common Hellenistic Gentile-Christian title for him) and their **love toward the saints** (see vv. 1 and 4).[6] The author, one should note, says he has heard these things; he himself has no firsthand knowledge of the recipients. **Faith in** may reflect the "believed" of v. 13; the **in** (*en*) is unusual and carries the sense of that in which faith rests.[7] An example of probable dependence surfaces when Eph. 1:15 is compared with Col. 1:4, 9.

Thanksgiving Proper (1:16-23)

Verse 16 is the actual, brief statement of thanksgiving that moves easily into a prayer of intercession that the gifts mentioned in the blessing would be further realized. God is addressed in language similar to vv. 1 and 3, but in addition he is called **the Father of glory,** which recalls the glory already discussed in vv. 6, 12, and 14. Ephesians often uses nouns as adjectives and it is likely that we have an example of that here; thus TEV's "the glorious Father" and NEB's "the all-glorious Father" (cf. Acts 7:2 and 1 Cor. 2:8).

The basic intercession is stated in v. 17*b*: **may give you a spirit of wisdom and of revelation in the knowledge of him.** The key is **knowledge,** which in Greek is an emphatic form that means full knowledge (cf. 1 Cor. 13:12); many scholars see a strong Gnostic element here. It is the **knowledge** that is true **wisdom** and it is a knowledge that, quite apart from intellectual knowledge, is a knowledge given only by revelation, that is, it is a knowledge which only God can give (cf. v. 9). Thus, while **spirit of wisdom** is not the Holy Spirit (contra TEV), that wisdom and knowledge are given through the Spirit. The goal is the knowledge of God (possibly of Christ) and the result of that knowledge and the further level of Christian maturity to which "Paul" invites the "Ephesians" is the further knowledge that is implied when one knows God, namely, the hope, the riches, and the power of God extended into the lives of believers.

All of these insights depend on the basis of Christian life, Baptism, to which the author refers in v. 18*a*, **having the eyes of your hearts enlightened.** Baptism is the moment of enlightenment in early Christianity; the perfect passive participial form of *enlighten* refers to a completed action with present active results. Therefore, "hope" orients the readers toward the future; they do not yet possess everything (see also 4:4). The **riches of his glorious inheritance in the saints** picks up themes already found in the blessing (vv. 6, 7, 12, 14; see also Col. 1:27). And **what is the immeasurable greatness of his power,** in typically redundant Ephesian fashion, completes the crescendo of intercessions by reminding the readers that the awesome **power** (*dynamis,* cf. English "dynamite") of God is "energized" (*energeia,* RSV **working**) **in us who believe.** That power, moreover, is the very same power and energy God used in raising Christ (v. 20). Thus, while of the greatest cosmic significance, God's power is at the same time active in believers.

Verses 20-23 are only loosely joined to the preceding. A number of scholars have identified a hymn in these verses; while that identification is unclear, it does appear that this section is strongly proclamatory and quite likely catechetical in nature (see also Rom. 8:34-39; 1 Peter 3:21-22). Christ, according to the formula, is resurrected and exalted. To be seated is to be in a position of authority. **At his right hand** refers to God's powerful side; **the heavenly places** has occurred already in v. 4 and refers to heaven.

Very likely the author has in mind Ps. 110:1, a popular proof text in early Christianity: "The Lord says to my lord: Sit at my right hand, till I make your enemies your footstool."[8] The psalm, a coronation psalm in its original setting, continues in v. 2: "The Lord sends forth from Zion your mighty scepter. Rule in the

midst of your foes!" And rule Christ does (v. 21)![9] The worldview
of v. 21 fits right into the popular mythology of the day in which
the heavenly spheres are populated by various entities. That mythology is also corrected, however, in that Christ is above every
one of the powers by which ancient humanity felt dominated (see
also Eph. 2:2; 3:10; 6:12; Rom. 8:38; 1 Cor. 15:24; cf. Col. 1:16
and 2:15). And that triumph and rule of Christ are effective now
and in any age to come. Christ is, therefore, the **head** (*kephalē;*
see v. 10, where the plan of God is to unite or sum up, *anake-*
phalaiōsasthai, all things in Christ). And he is **the head over all**
things (*ta panta*), that is, the universe (again, see v. 10). In this
climactic conclusion to chap. 1 Christ is viewed as the ruler of
the various powers which populate the heavens, but he is also
understood as the very ruler of the *kosmos.* Once again the author
may be reflecting the popular view that the world was a huge
body, with heaven or the universal mind as the head. All of this
exalted Christology is, however, to be understood from an ec-
clesiological perspective, for Christ's rulership is carried out **for**
the church.

With the term **church** (*ekklēsia*) we come to another OT word
that has been reapplied to the people of God in Christ. In the
Septuagint (the Greek OT), **church** is used to translate the Hebrew *qahal* or "assembly," a term that was applied to the whole
people of Israel in assembly. In Ephesians, in fact, **church** always
means the universal church and never the individual local congregation (3:10, 21; 5:23, 24, 25, 27, 29, 32). The perspective in v.
22 is without doubt universal, as is seen in v. 23 where the church
is more closely defined. The connective link at the beginning of
v. 23 is stronger than **which.** It carries this sense: ". . . the church
which, in fact, is his body." The passage seems reminiscent of
Paul in Rom. 12:4-8 and 1 Cor. 12:12-31, but in Ephesians the
distinctive view of the deutero-Paulines is evident, in that Christ
is the *head* of the body. The body is further designated as his
fulness. To understand the thought here we need to look at the
Colossian raw material:[10] "He is the head of the body, the church;
. . . For in him all the fulness of God was pleased to dwell" (1:18-

19). God fills Christ; Christ, in turn, fills the church in a special
way because it is there that his will and plan are most fully realized. We can, in fact, talk of an ever greater "filling" of the
believer (3:19; 5:18; cf. 4:15-16), although the identity of believer
and God is not confused. The church, in sum, is the body which
Christ fills, in which his blessings and his power are effective.
Throughout the section the author seems to argue with Gnosticism, in which "fulness" is the higher spirit world of the aeons/
ages and in which redeemed and redeemer are identified. While
2:1 introduces a new section, there is no formal ending to the
prayer until 3:21.

■ Narration: God's Love (2:1-10)

The author continues in 2:1-10 the direction established in
chap. 1. Thus the first half of chap. 2 builds on the concept of
the resurrection in 1:20; what God did for Christ he also does for
the ones who believe in him. In addition, by means of a then-
now pattern the author reminds his readers of what God has done
specifically for them. By reminding them of God's work he continues to lay the indicative foundation for the imperatives to follow. This section has, therefore, a function quite close to that of
the narrative section outlined by Aristotle, *Ars Rhetorica* 3.16.1-
2, 8-10 (see also the Introduction, above). Emphasis on the ex-
travagant richness of God's grace continues throughout these
verses, as does emphasis on the collective nature of salvation.

Statement of the Gentiles' Condition (2:1-2)

Our analysis is to some extent artificial, for the Greek sentence
that begins in v. 1 continues all the way through v. 7. There is,
moreover, no main or independent verb until v. 5, despite the
RSV's insertion into v. 1 of **he made alive.** What the author does
is to begin a thought in v. 1 (**and you . . . when you were dead**

through the trespasses and sins) only to move in a somewhat
different direction until he resumes in v. 5 the same initial
thought, although in the first person plural rather than the second
person plural of v. 1. Verses 1 and 5 are likely dependent on Col.
2:13, although the Colossian reference to uncircumcision is omitted in Ephesians (but see 2:11).

The **and** both connects our section with what has preceded it
and marks a new section. As elsewhere in Ephesians, the exact
identification of **you** must remain open; this study prefers Gentiles as the antecedent because of the overall context (1:13-14;
2:11-13), but that identification must remain tentative (cf. the
description of Gentile behavior in 4:17-19). In any event, **you
were dead through the trespasses and sins in which you once
walked.** The author speaks of a real death, even if it is not a
biological death. While with TEV and Phillips we can talk of it
as a "spiritual" death, we would do better to call it "a realised
eschatological conception of death."[11] That is, pre-Christian existence or existence apart from Christ is a life in which the person
"exists" as though already eternally dead (i.e., outside a relationship with God in Christ). It is such a realistic conception that
only a resurrection can turn it around (vv. 5-6; see also 5:14; Col.
2:13; 1 Tim. 5:6; Rev. 3:1; John 5:24; 1 John 3:14). The cause of
death is listed as **trespasses and sins.** While there is some distinction between the terms, the author is most probably giving
us another example of hendiadys, a literary device by which two
nouns are joined by "and" where in English we would have a
noun and a modifier. Of greater importance is the fact that of the
61 occurrences of "sin" in the undisputed letters of Paul, 54 occurrences are in the singular. Of the other seven occurrences,
all but one (Rom. 7:5) are in credal formulas or OT allusions or
quotations. The plural in Eph. 2:1 thus is an unusual usage of
the term. On the other hand, only the plural is found in the
Pastoral Epistles (1 Tim. 5:22, 24; 2 Tim. 3:6).

Walked refers in the Bible as well as in other literature to one's
ethical walk of life. The Gentiles **once** or "formerly" walked **fol-**

lowing the course of this world. RSV translates **following** from the favorite Ephesian term *kata,* "according to." The world **course** is the Greek word *aiōn,* meaning "age." It likely carries that common Pauline meaning here, that is, "this age," or "the age of evil" (see Rom. 12:2; 1 Cor. 1:20; 2:6; 3:18; Gal. 1:4). To live according to this age is also to live according to the devil, **the prince of the power of the air.** Non-Christian humanity is not only dead, it is also ruled by malevolent supernatural forces which, we read later, continue to harass believers (6:11-12). The devil's realm is in the air, that region above earth but below heaven. It is his spirit that is **at work in the sons of disobedience. Sons of disobedience** is a Semitic phrase paralleled at Qumran (1QH 5:25; 1QS 1:10; 3:21; etc.); it lists disobedience to God as the chief characteristic of those so designated. The verb **work** also appears in 1:11 and 1:20; the noun form is in 1:19. In each case it is used of God and his activity among people. That kind of activity is, however, not limited to God. There is clearly another one at work, the one who in 4:27 and 6:11 is called the devil.

Statement of the Jews' Condition and of the Condition of All (2:3*ab*)

The author shifts person in v. 3 to **we.** If Gentiles are meant in vv. 1-2, the natural contrast would be to Jews in v. 3. It is possible, though, that the author has simply moved from addressing the recipients as separate from himself to including himself in his remarks. In any event, he quickly passes to a concern for all of humanity, **we all.** The former life is again emphasized; it is characterized by the passions that stem from the flesh and from **following the desires of body and mind.** The point becomes clear when we discover that RSV's **desires** is the same Greek word used in 1:1, 5, 9, and 11 for the "will" of God. To live in the desires of the flesh, therefore, is to live according to one's own will and not according to the will of God.

Result (2:3*c*)

The result of such desiring is a negative childhood totally the opposite of God's will (see 1:5). Instead of love and grace, God's eschatological wrath comes into play, for **children of wrath** carries the sense of "children *deserving* of wrath." And thus the Jews become like the rest (**of mankind** is not in the Greek), that is, like the Gentiles (see also 1 Thess. 4:13). In a nutshell, the author has summarized what Paul developed in Rom. 1:18—3:18.

The Divine "But" (2:4-10)

Against all of humanity's desiring and self-will the author quite simply writes, **but God.** Dramatically and eloquently he almost sings of the graceful activity of God; indeed, many scholars have identified a quoted hymn in vv. 4-7, to which 5*b* and possibly 4*b* have been added (others include v. 10 in the hymn). God is above all characterized by the term **mercy.** This mercy is so over-whelming that it can only be talked about in terms of wealth. The actual term **rich** occurs only here in Ephesians, but the noun form has already occurred in 1:7 and 18 and it will appear again in 2:7; 3:8; and 3:16. But why does God act in mercy? Simply **out of the great love with which he loved us.** God's love is the answer. He loves—period (see also 1:4).

The depth of that love of God is indicated in v. 5 when the author finally returns to the unfinished thought of v. 1 (although he does it in the first person plural): precisely at the point of our death, when "we" through our self-will had, in a sense, com-mitted suicide, precisely at that point God **made us alive together with Christ, . . . raised us up with him, and made us sit with him in the heavenly places.** Here the author explicitly builds on 1:20: just as God's power has been active in Christ so now it is active in us. The parallel activity is expressed by the three main verbs of vv. 5 and 6: **made us alive together with Christ, raised us up with him,** and **made us sit with him.** The three verbs, with the exception of "sit with" in Luke 22:55, occur only in Ephesians and Colossians.

When did all of this take place? We would naturally think of the future, but each of the verbs mentioned is aorist tense (completed action in past time). In addition, the verb in the interjection of v. 5 (**by grace you have been saved**) is in the perfect tense. When we look for a completed past action we find, once again, Baptism; when we recall the baptismal material in chap. 1, as well as the parallels in Col. 2:12 and Rom. 6:1-11, our hypothesis is confirmed. To be baptized into Christ is to share with him fully, even to the point of speaking of a present-tense resurrection. One scholar even speculates that early Christian Baptism may have included some sort of enthronement rite.[12] Certainly many religious people strove to ascend to heaven by ascetic practices; perhaps Ephesians wants to say that such an ascent is given freely by God. We may again see a Gnostic milieu peeking through. The differences between Ephesians and the undisputed letters on these issues have already been mentioned (pp. 14f. of the Introduction). Paul never says that he participates in the resurrection of Christ. Resurrection is clearly future in 1 Corinthians 15; Phil. 3:11; Rom. 6:5-8; 8:18-25. For that matter, salvation is also a future concept in Paul; Paul, with one exception, uses the present tense with a continuative meaning ("is being saved") or the future. Rom. 8:24, the one exception, is really no exception, for "saved" is there qualified by hope. In Eph. 2:5 and 8, on the other hand, the author uses the perfect tense. Salvation is realized, not expected (see also 2 Tim. 1:9 and Titus 3:5).

The purpose of the believers' enthronement is to function as a sort of grand audiovisual display or evidence in the final eschatological lawsuit on the day of judgment (v. 7). **In the coming ages** may refer literally to the ages of time to follow; the phrase could also mean "among the coming (or attacking) aeons," referring to hostile forces evident especially in Gnostic mythology. God, on that interpretation, would use the saved as his chief piece of evidence against his enemies. Verse 8, by way of explanation, repeats the principle of salvation which has already been interjected into v. 5, although with the addition of **through faith.**

This principle of salvation is itself, in turn, explained by two contrasts. **And this** (the whole fact of salvation) **is not your own doing, it is the gift of God.** Salvation is not earned; it is given, which is what saved by grace means. The second contrast carries on the thought of the first: **not because of works, lest any man should boast.** Boasting is a favorite Pauline theme (Rom. 3:27; 1 Cor. 1:29, 31; 3:21); its fundamental thought is that humans cannot boast before God. Verse 10 closes the section by specifying why in fact no one may boast; **For we are his workmanship,** literally "his thing," what God has made. Almost ironically, however, the relationship with good works is immediately brought to bear. The new humanity, the humanity **created in Christ Jesus** (see 2:15 and 4:24), is created precisely for good works prepared by God. The good works do not themselves save but they are the outcome of the new creation effected in Christ (see also Gal. 6:15 and 2 Cor. 5:17). It is now the very nature of the Christian to do good works; good works are part of the new life God has given, as once again God has brought order out of the chaos of human sin. The author ends where he began the section, namely, with **walk**— but what a different walk, to be detailed in 4:17—6:20! He turns now, however, to another reminder.

■ Admonition to Remember (2:11-22)

The genre of Ephesians as a type of remembering literature is nowhere more in evidence than it is in the present section. The section opens with a negative remembrance of who the addressees formerly were—Gentiles totally cut off from God (vv. 11-12); the opening verses return to the theme already enunciated in v. 1. In v. 13 the readers are called to a positive remembrance of God's saving action, which is elucidated by a hymn of praise to Christ (vv. 14-18). The final portion of the admonition draws out the implications of the preceding verses for present life in the church (vv. 19-22).

Negative Remembrance (2:11-12)

The author begins with **therefore,** as a way to resume the remembering begun in v. 1 and as a method of transition. The verb **remember** is in the present tense; it carries the sense of "keep on remembering," not only right now but always. And what are they to remember? They are to remember who and what they were. They were **Gentiles in the flesh,** from the perspective of the Jews (the historical Paul has simply "the Gentiles"; he never adds "in the flesh"). Their derisive nickname was **the uncircumcision,** a name given to them by those for whom circumcision was the sign of a covenantal relationship with God. (Note, however, what may be an implicit criticism of Jewish **circumcision, which is made in the flesh by hands.** Cf. on spiritual circumcision Col. 2:11; Rom. 2:29; and Phil. 3:3.) The Gentiles were, moreover, **separated from Christ,** an especially negative remembrance for the author when we recall his extreme emphasis on "in Christ." Second, they were excluded from Israel. **Alienated** may carry the sense of having once had a relationship with Israel; the meaning rather is that the Gentiles were estranged or excluded from Israel, that is, from the people of God (see also 4:18 and Col. 1:21). Being thus excluded the Gentiles were **strangers to the covenants** and the promise, with the result that they had **no hope** and, to express the thought in its ultimate form, they were **without God in the world. Without God** translates the Greek *atheos,* literally "atheist"; the connotation here is that they did not know God (the term *atheos* occurs only here in the NT; it does not occur in the Septuagint or Apocrypha). The Gentiles in vv. 1-2 were to remember their alienation in terms of sin; here they are to remember that religiously they were outsiders.

Positive Remembrance (2:13)

But now in Christ: these words contain the author's theology in one brief phrase. Similar in structure and content to v. 4, the phrase is an emphatic contrast to the former state of the Gentiles. The change is effected **in Christ,** as always in Ephesians. The next words, as well as v. 15, likely reflect Isa. 57:19, "Peace, peace, to the far and to the near, says the Lord." Originally the verse referred to Jews in exile and Jews at home; it had been used for some time in Judaism, however, to speak of Gentiles (the far) and Jews (the near), especially in discussions of Gentiles converting to Judaism. "To bring near" is to make someone part of the people of God (also at Qumran, although not of Gentiles, e.g., 1QS 11.13 and 1QH 14.13-14); in Ephesians that inclusion is made possible **in the blood of Christ,** the primary reference being to the cross, although an oblique reference to circumcision is not impossible (see v. 11).

Hymn of Praise to Christ (2:14-18)

The author digresses a bit by including a section on praise to the Christ who has brought the Gentiles near. The section is set apart by the **for** of v. 14 and the **so then** of v. 19, which resumes the thought temporarily left behind in v. 13. Indications of a quoted hymn are the sudden shift in v. 14 from **you** to **us** (**you** crops up in v. 17 and resumes in v. 19), the participial and relative clauses which are typical in ancient hymns, and the parallel constructions of v. 14*b* with 15*a* and 15*b* with 16. The material also begins with the redeemer figure and ends with the Father, as does the hymn in Phil. 2:6-11; in content vv. 14-18 are quite similar to Col. 1:15-22, especially vv. 20-22.

The theme of the hymn is stated in the first line: **he is our peace.** Christ is himself the promised messianic peace (Isa. 57:19 again; also 9:6 and 52:7). In himself the twofold peace of the hymn is given: peace between Jew and Gentile (a usage of peace unique to Ephesians) and peace between humanity and God (cf. Rom. 5:1; John 14:27; 16:33; 20:19-21; 20:26). The first peacemaking activity of Christ is that he **has made us both one,** which rather clearly refers to Jew and Gentile, the contrast between which has been a constant theme in the chapter. The **one** assumes a particular importance when viewed in light of the great verse on unity, Gal. 3:28: "There is neither Jew nor Greek, there is neither slave nor free, there is neither male nor female; for you are all one in Christ Jesus."[13] Out of the two basic divisions of humanity Christ creates **one new man in place of the two** (v. 15). **One new man** is conversion language. Christians are, in Pauline and later theology, a new humanity (a better translation for *anthrōpos* than **man**), a sort of third race which is constitutive for the new creation in Christ (on new creation see on v. 10 above and Eph. 4:24).[14] The new humanity is no longer determined by racial or national distinctions; it is now determined and directed in Christ.

Of interest is that the **us** of the RSV translation of v. 14 is not present in Greek, which has led some commentators to argue that the original version of this hymn referred not to the unity of Jew and Gentile but to the Gnostic concern for the overcoming of the opposition between the physical and the spiritual. According to this interpretation the **dividing wall** that was broken was the wall separating the aeons of the *plērōma* ("fulness"; aeons or *plērōma* appear in 1:10, 21, 23; 2:2, 7; 3:9, 11, 19, 21; 4:13) from the earthly world. The wall is broken as the redeemer returns to the heavenly world, defeating all enemies along the way. The removal of the dividing wall thus means access to the true God. If that interpretation has any validity, then the author in taking over the hymn has radically historicized it. We can identify that historicization in the use made in the Ephesian context of **the dividing wall of hostility** (v. 14). While a few would understand the phrase as referring to the curtain that divided the Holy of Holies from the rest of the Jewish temple, most see here a reference to the temple wall which separated the court of the Gentiles from the inner areas. Gentiles could be killed if they entered the portions of the temple reserved exclusively for Jews. Those reserved portions did in fact include the inner temple, where God himself was thought to dwell. The dividing wall thus expresses the twofold division of the overall hymn: division between people and division from God. The poignancy of the image comes into focus when we recall the destruction of the temple in Jerusalem in 70—prior to the writing of Ephesians. Christ eliminates that division **by abolishing in his flesh the law of**

commandments and ordinances. The use of **abolish** is especially radical when compared with the historical Paul, and the radicality is even greater when one realizes that **the law** refers to the entirety of the Jewish law. At least one scholar has therefore argued that **the law** itself was **the dividing wall.**[15] Christ abolishes the law, it is to be noted, **in his flesh.** That phrase needs to be understood in light of v. 16, **through the cross.** It is the death of Christ on the cross that reconciles both Jew and Gentile as well as God and humanity (see Col. 1:20, 22; 2 Cor. 5:18-20; Rom. 5:10).

In one body in v. 16 most likely refers to the body of Christ, the church, which was already discussed in 1:22-23 (see also 3:6). The final phrase of v. 16 is actually much stronger than the RSV translation. The Greek reads, "having killed the enmity in him." That is, at his own death Jesus kills (cf. Gal. 3:10-14). And what he kills is the hostility, the enmity, the hate existing among people and between people and God. And so the proclamation (better than RSV's **preached**) of Christ can be summarized as **peace,** a peace proclaimed both to the **far off** (Gentiles) and to the **near** (Jews; see v. 13; the author combines Isa. 52:7 with 57:19). It is futile to search for one specific moment of proclamation. Jesus himself is the peace (v. 14), and his entire life, ministry, death, and resurrection are the proclamation of that same peace with which believers are to shoe their feet (6:15; indeed chaps. 4–6 deal with how peace and reconciliation are lived out in everyday community life). The hymn concludes with an early trinitarian statement on the result of Christ's work. The key term is **access in one Spirit to the Father.** In ancient Near Eastern courts the "accessor" or chamberlain (*prosagōgēs*) was the official who controlled access to the king. In such a way Jesus provides **access to the Father** for both Jew and Gentile (see also 3:12 and Rom. 5:2; "one Spirit" occurs in 4:4). **Father** is a favorite Ephesian term for God (1:2, 3, 17; 2:18; 3:14; 4:6; 5:20; 6:23).

Ecclesiastical Implications (2:19-22)

Verse 19 resumes the thought of vv. 12-13; **so then** *(ara oun)* is in Greek especially used to begin a summary. In this case the summary views the discussion from a church perspective. **No longer** are the Gentiles **strangers and sojourners,** that is, non-resident aliens with no rights (**strangers**) and resident aliens with limited rights (**sojourners;** one should not make too much of the distinction, since we probably have simply another example of hendiadys). Now the Gentiles are **fellow citizens with the saints. Fellow citizens** is a cognate of "commonwealth" in v. 12; **saints** probably refers to the people of Israel, although it may refer to Christians as the new people of God. Some see a reference to angels. **Members of the household of God** means the same as the previous phrase, with **members of the household** (*oikeioi*) being a cognate of **sojourners** (*paroikoi*). The household is **built upon the foundation of the apostles and prophets,** a statement quite different from 1 Cor. 3:11, where Jesus Christ is the foundation (cf. Rev. 21:14; on the image of the church as a building see Matt. 16:18 and especially 1 Peter 2:4-10, which contains many parallels to our passage). The statement may be an indication of early catholicism, in which Gnostic opponents are combatted by appeal to the traditions and doctrines of the church. **Prophets** most likely refers to Christian prophets rather than OT prophets (note 3:5 and 4:11). The cornerstone of the building is Christ Jesus (see also Matt. 21:42; 1 Peter 2:4-8; and Acts 4:11, all of which are based on Ps. 118:22 and quite possibly Isa. 28:16), that is, the stone placed in the foundation at the corner where the two walls come together; it is that stone which gives direction and shape to the building. And so it is in him that the building composed of people not only is **joined together,** which means literally to "harmonize together" or to "fit together," it also **grows,** since it is a dynamic human building in which the growth is ongoing (see 4:15-16). What the building is becoming is **a holy temple in the Lord.** The Greek word used here for **temple** (*naos*) means the inner sanctuary, the Holy of Holies, where God meets his people. Now, our author says, the church itself is that place of meeting (cf. vv. 14 and 15) and, lest the Ephesians forget, they are reminded that they are being **built into it** (divine passive, as in v. 20) to be in fact that **dwelling place of God in the Spirit.**

(For similar statements about the community as a building and temple see 1QS 8:4-10; 9:5-6; 1QH 6:25-27; 7:8-9.)

■ Prayer of the Apostle (3:1-21)

Once we leave the broad outline of Ephesians (chaps. 1–3 are praise and proclamation, chaps. 4–6 are exhortation) we encounter the difficulty of discerning just how all the various sections fit together. That difficulty is especially evident in chap. 3.

There seem to be at least three functions fulfilled by this chapter. The first function is that of recalling Paul's ministry; in the digression that extends from vv. 2-13, the author reminds his readers of the apostle's message and ministry. Such sections are typical in early portions of other Pauline letters also (Rom. 1:13-15; 2 Cor. 1:8—2:13; Gal. 1:11—2:21; Phil. 1:12-26; 1 Thess. 2:1—3:8). It is noteworthy that, in a letter which we have styled a remembrance or reminder, there is a specific section to remind readers of what they have heard about Paul's proclamation and apostleship (see v. 2), especially since he is not personally known by the recipients.

The second function of chap. 3 is closely related to the first function: the author needs to establish the right of Paul to address the recipients at all; he meets that need by listing Paul's credentials as a way of authenticating his apostolic authority. Such a goal is normal for the part of the epideictic speech called the *exordium*, which is designed " . . . chiefly to project a character for the orator, an *ethos*, which would persuade the audience to trust him."[16] Often the *exordium* reminds the recipients of the speaker's authority, as does our present chapter.

The third function is to complete the prayer begun in 1:16-17 but never concluded: vv. 14-21 finally draw to an end that portion of the letter. In developing his thoughts the author is heavily dependent on Col. 1:23-28 (Mitton, 118, has a chart of the dependencies); the author also continues his practice of repeating and deepening themes developed earlier, in this case further developing thoughts expressed in 2:11-22 (cf. 3:1 and 2:11; 3:3 and 2:19; 3:5 and 2:20; 3:6 and 2:12; 3:12 and 2:18).

Identification of the Suppliant (3:1)

For this reason provides another loose connection between two sections. The author has just concluded a discussion of the inclusion of the Gentiles; he now turns to Paul's place in God's plan of salvation, and so it is **for this reason,** because of the message of God's salvation for all people, that Paul is imprisoned. The words **I, Paul** are emphatic; they are themselves an assertion of authority and they are in a sense underlined by the repeated uses in this section of **I, me,** and **my** (vv. 1, 2, 3, 4, 7, 8, 13). This Paul is a prisoner; the Greek term means literally "one who is in bonds." The term occurs also in 4:1 and Philemon 1 and 9 (cf. Eph. 6:20). In each case Paul is a prisoner of Christ Jesus or a prisoner for the Lord. Paul is thus a prisoner neither by accident nor because he has maliciously broken society's rules. His imprisonment has a purpose. Elsewhere Paul speaks of his bonds (Phil. 1:7, 13, 14, 17; Col. 4:18). Thus the four letters in which Paul is "one who is in bonds" or in which there is reference to his bonds are often grouped together as the "captivity" or "prison letters." He is, moreover, imprisoned **on behalf of you Gentiles.** The prepositional phrase **on behalf of** translates the Greek term *hyper.* In the pillar epistles it is a frequent preposition used to summarize the work of Christ ("he died on behalf of us"); the preposition is used of Christ (Eph. 5:2, 25) as well as of Paul (3:1, 13; Col. 1:24; cf. 2 Tim. 2:10). Paul is not, certainly, to be ranked with Christ, but in Ephesians he is an absolutely crucial figure for the spread of the gospel to the Gentiles; indeed he is viewed in Ephesians as *the* preeminent apostle to the Gentiles.

Digression on Paul's Credentials and His Gospel (3:2-13)

Description of the Message Assumed Heard (3:2-6)

That the "Paul" of our document was not personally known to

his readers is made quite clear in v. 2 (see also 1:15). The author finds it necessary to remind the readers of what he assumes they have heard, namely, the center of the gospel and Paul's place in its spread. The word **stewardship** in v. 2 translates the Greek word *oikonomia*, which was used in 1:10 with reference to Christ; it there carried more the sense of "plan," as it also does in 3:9. Paul is thus a steward who is part of God's plan of salvation, since to him God's grace was given **for you,** that is, for the Gentiles (see Rom. 15:15; 1:5; 12:3; as well as Eph. 3:7-8). It is interesting that in Gal. 1:13-17 Paul reminds his readers not of his special office but of his former life in Judaism; we may well have in Ephesians a more idealized picture of the apostle.

The content of the grace given to Paul is **the mystery,** a mystery which **was made known to me by revelation** (v. 3). **Was made known** is a divine passive, that is, a use of the passive voice to indicate God as the implied subject of the verb. That judgment is confirmed in the words **by revelation,** which resume a theme already introduced in 1:17. Paul talks in his undisputed letters about the revelation given to him (most notably Gal. 1:12 and 16), but the closest parallel is Rom. 16:25-27, which not only contains the same construction ("by revelation") but which also has the word so important to Ephesians, "mystery." Different ancient manuscripts place what in the RSV is printed as Rom. 16:25-27 at other points in Romans (after 14:23 and 15:33); its position as part of the original copy of Romans is thus textually suspect. Some scholars even feel that Rom. 16:25-27 was written to Ephesus! The "mystery" is the inclusion of the Gentiles (v. 6), and therefore the final words of v. 3, **as I have written briefly,** refer to his previous discussion of the Gentiles in chap. 2. **The mystery** (also properly translated "secret" in TEV and Phillips), however, was *not* previously **made known** (v. 5; same verb as in v. 3). It has only now been revealed (cf. **revelation** in v. 3) and the revelation of the mystery has come only to the **apostles, by** means of **the Spirit.** As in 2:20, the **prophets** are contemporary Christian prophets and not the OT prophets; indeed, the mystery was, implicitly, hidden even from the OT giants of the faith.

One might well question whether the historical Paul would have designated the **apostles and prophets** as **holy.** For that matter, a number of scholars have argued that v. 5*b* is either a later gloss or perhaps a quotation cited by the author, since in v. 3 it is only to Paul that the mystery has been made known. The content of the mystery is stated in v. 6: the inclusion of the Gentiles. That thought is even more dramatically developed in the Greek, which could be translated, "that the Gentiles might be fellow heirs and fellow body members and fellow partakers of the promise." The unity of Jew and Gentile is especially indicated by the words translated with **fellow,** which resume earlier themes: on inheritance see 1:14 and 1:18, on **body** see 1:23, and on **promise** see 2:12, where the Gentiles are strangers to the promise. God's mysterious plan has overcome that division by means of the gospel, the good news about Jesus the Christ (see 1:13).

Paul's Credentials (3:7-13)

Verse 7 in Greek is more closely linked to v. 6 than the RSV indicates; the verse is, in fact, a transition from discussing Paul's gospel to discussing Paul's credentials. Quite significant is the basis of Paul's ministry (indeed, one could argue, of all ministry); the basis for ministry is the free gift of God's grace, a grace that comes through the working of God's power (see 1:11; 1:19-20; 3:20). And grace results not in an office to be filled but a ministry to be carried out, a ministry that may even result in prison (v. 1). That ministry of Paul's is detailed in v. 8; Paul is **to preach** the gospel **to the Gentiles.** The overwhelming nature of the grace is indicated by "Paul's" strongly negative self-assessment. In 1 Cor. 15:9 Paul is the least of the apostles; here he is **the very least of all the saints. Very least** is an odd construction, and this in itself indicates the weight the author wants it to have. The message does not depend on Paul, but on God. Paul's commission

is to preach **the unsearchable riches of Christ.** We have encountered **riches** and related words before (1:7, 18; 2:4, 7; also
in 3:16). They are **unsearchable** not in the sense of being hidden
but in the sense of their vastness and unending nature.

The other aspect of Paul's ministry is **to make all men see what
is the plan of the mystery hidden in God. To make . . . see** is
the Greek verb "enlighten," which is also used in 1:18, where
"riches" likewise occurs. **The plan of the mystery** is the very
inclusion of the Gentiles; this plan was previously **hidden** (see v.
5) **for ages in God,** which could also legitimately be translated
as "hidden from the aeons by God," thus giving the phrase the
more mythological interpretation we have noted in other places.
Indeed, "enlighten," "mystery," "plan," and "aeons" were common Gnostic concepts. Such an opponent could explain the sudden introduction at the end of v. 10 of God as creator, since
Gnosticism so sharply distinguished between the God of creation
and the God of salvation. The Gnostic possibility is increased in
v. 10 with the introduction of **principalities and powers in the
heavenly places,** to whom the church is to make known God's
wisdom.

The church is conceived as a cosmic entity with cosmic re-
sponsibility, which it carries out in part through its witness as a
unified body composed of both Jews and Gentiles (on vv. 8-10
see Col. 1:26-28). It functions according to God's eternal purpose
(v. 11), a purpose or plan God has carried out in Christ Jesus (see
especially 1:7-14). Christ Jesus is further identified as the one **in
whom we have boldness and confidence of access.** The thought
resumes another earlier image, this time from 2:18. In Christ
people not only have access to the Father; they are also able to
hold up their heads in his presence. **Through our faith in him**
could also be translated "through his [Christ's] faithfulness." Having once more reminded the readers of what God had done for
them, the author concludes with an appeal that they not become
discouraged because of Paul's **suffering** which, after all, is a glorious thing (cf. 1:6, 12, 14).[17]

Prayer Resumed (3:14-21)

The author begins v. 14 with the same words he used to introduce v. 1, **for this reason.** By repeating those words he indicates that he is resuming the prayer begun at the beginning of the chapter but temporarily neglected because of the "digression" in vv. 2-13 (which is actually well planned). In light of his mission to the Gentiles and in light of the revelation to him of God's plan, the apostolic figure prays for an ever-ascending array of gifts to be given the readers: strength through the Spirit, the indwelling of Christ, power to comprehend, ability to know the love of Christ, and, finally, being filled with God's fulness. The prayer concludes in vv. 20-21 with a doxology.

Since the suppliant has been identified in v. 1, the author proceeds immediately in v. 14 with an indication of the act of supplication (**I bow my knees**). While the more usual position for prayer in Judaism and early Christianity was standing (Mark 11:25; Luke 18:11, 13), "bending the knee" was by no means unknown (1 Kings 8:54; Dan. 6:10; Luke 22:41; Acts 7:60; cf. Phil. 2:10). It is quite likely that the author meant a prone position, with the suppliant's face on the ground. The object of the supplication is the Father, who is mentioned in every chapter of Ephesians. The Father is praised in the language of creation (v. 15) as the one who names **every family in heaven and on earth.** The creative aspect of the thought is evident in the naming, which is itself a powerful creative act (Gen. 1:5, for example). The creation motif may also be present in the Greek wordplay of Father (*patēr*) and family (*patria*). But who is referred to in v. 15? The translation by Phillips speaks of "all fatherhood," a meaning for the term *patria* unknown in other Greek literature and therefore highly suspect. The NEB, in a note, suggests "his whole family," referring presumably to the church, but the Greek grammatical construction precludes that translation. We seem to have a reference to the angels, who are the family in heaven (various rabbinic texts), and to the multiplicity of human nations and races on earth. God is therefore praised for being the creator of all (it is unlikely that the opposing powers of 3:10 and 1:21 are included); once again the author may be combatting the Gnostic divisions, heavenly/earthly and redemption/ creation, as well as indicating yet again that the message is for all people.

The actual requests begin in v. 16, but first the author reminds his readers of the basis on which God can be approached at all: **according to the riches of his glory. Riches** and **glory** are, by this point in our study, well-established Ephesian themes. The first request is that the Father would **grant you to be strengthened with might through his Spirit in the inner man.** The verb "strengthen" occurs only here in Ephesians, but the related noun does occur in 1:19 and 6:10. The author, as we have repeatedly seen, likes to use related forms in this way; his method, incidentally perhaps, also serves to tie together the entire work. The mode of strengthening is the Spirit and what is to be strengthened is **the inner man,** which refers to the reflective and responsive "part" or aspect of the human being (on **inner man** see 2 Cor. 4:16 and Rom. 7:22).[18] A parallel request is made in v. 17, which, like v. 16, contains an infinitive ("to dwell"; RSV **may dwell**), a prepositional phrase begun with **through,** and the location of the action (**in your hearts**). The two requests may in fact interpret each other: the indwelling of Christ is the way the believers are strengthened; **through faith** (from humanity's side presumably) and **through** the **Spirit** God effects the strengthening; and it is in the heart/inner person that the strengthening and indwelling occur (see John 14:23 and 2 Cor. 6:16). Already in 2:22 the author has used the same vocabulary to speak of God's dwelling in his people. Is there in 3:17 an implicit claim for the divinity of Christ, who also dwells in people? Perhaps. What is clear is that in vv. 14-17 there is an incipient trinitarian character to the prayer.

The next request assumes a rootage (agricultural image) and a grounding or foundation (construction image) **in love,** another Ephesian concept present in each chapter. The request is once more for a strengthening or empowering (the related noun form occurs in 1:19 and 6:10), but this time for the ability **to comprehend with all the saints what is the breadth and length and height**

and depth (v. 18). Of what, the reader wants to ask. Most scholars opt for **the love of Christ** from v. 19; that is, the request is that the readers would understand the awesomeness of that love (see TEV, NEB, and Phillips). Others, building on the language of foundation and indwelling common to chaps. 2 and 3, see a reference here to the Jerusalem temple (perhaps spiritualized; cf. the Dead Sea Scrolls). Others identify a reference to the measurements of the universe and hence of **the saints** as angels, rather than human believers. In all cases, though, the point is to emphasize **the love of Christ which surpasses knowledge** (v. 19), perhaps an implicit comment against the Gnostic claim for special knowledge (cf. 1 Cor. 8:1; 12–14). Gnostic influence may also be seen in the final words of the supplication, **that you may be filled with all the fulness of God,** which is the result of knowing Christ's love (contrast Col. 1:19). **Filled** and **fulness** are two other standard Ephesian themes and refer to the presence of God in the lives of his people (2:22 and 3:17). Yet the basis of Christian life remains the love revealed in Christ; all other knowledge is secondary.

The doxology finally concludes the prayer begun in 3:14—or was it 3:1? Or 1:15? Or even 1:3? In typical doxological fashion the author finishes his prayer with equally typical Ephesian emphases on the overwhelming nature of God's activity (v. 20) and an ascription of glory to God (v. 21). The author subtly draws the readers into the prayer's ending by shifting to **us** and **we.** The locus of the doxology is **in the church and in Christ Jesus,** which have remained the two foci throughout the first half of the letter. Having carefully laid the theological foundation, the author now turns to the practical implications of such a worldview.

■ Exhortation/Paraenesis (4:1—6:20)

A clear shift occurs with the very first word of chap. 4; in Greek that word is **beg** (RSV), or better, "exhort, encourage, entreat" (*parakalō*). This technical verb introduces the longest division of Ephesians; that division extends almost to the end of the document. The exhortation (paraenesis) contained in 4:1—6:20 is quite

similar in structure to the exhortative sections of 1 Thess. 4:1—
5:22; Gal. 5:1—6:10; Phil. 2:12-29; 4:2-6; Rom. 12:1—15:13; and
Col. 3:1—4:6. Theologically, the order of material in Ephesians
(as well as elsewhere) is quite important: first the indicative, the
statement of God's activity, is developed; only after the indicative
base has been laid does the author develop in a systematic way
the ethical response which is based on the indicative. The small
word **therefore** thus assumes an unusually pivotal function, for
it ties together all the author has written in the doxological-doc-
trinal section with what he will write in the paraenetical or so-
called "practical" section. Just as the first three chapters have
been concerned with the universal implications of the gospel, so
the last three chapters are concerned with ethical implications
that determine every aspect of the church's life, in both its communal and in its more individualistic ethical responses. Every
relationship and every activity are to be scrutinized by the revelation of Christ. Thus the implications of the cosmic Christ and
the cosmic church are worked out for the mundane lives of God's
people. Christians may in some way be raised and exalted with
Christ (2:6) but they also live on earth.

Introduction (4:1*a*)

The author once more reminds the readers of who Paul is: **I
. . ., a prisoner for the Lord,** literally, a prisoner *in* the Lord
(see also 3:1). The repetition of this designation adds force to the
exhortation; "Paul" speaks with the authority of one who is in
prison because of his loyalty to the Lord, and therefore his ethical
directives carry a particular weight.

Basic Exhortation (4:1*b*-6)

The basic exhortation is stated in v. 1*b* and then further developed in vv. 2-6: **I . . . beg you to lead a life worthy of the
calling to which you have been called.** The key terms are **lead
a life, worthy,** and **calling. Lead a life** translates the Greek *per-
ipateō,* which means "to walk" and which earlier in the biblical

and Greek philosophical writings had assumed the ethical meaning of walking one's life in a certain way. The term is used throughout Ephesians (2:2, 10; 4:17; 5:2, 8, 15). The usage of the term in chap. 2 indicates the clear ties between the first and second halves of the letter; 2:10 especially foreshadows the exhortative section. The second key term is **worthy.** Originally the term meant "bringing up the other beam of the scales," "bringing into equilibrium."[19] It therefore refers to a correspondence or balancing. Hence our passage could be translated, "live in a way corresponding to your calling," which again is quite reminiscent of 2:10.[20] The final term is actually used twice: once as a noun (**calling**) and once as a verb (**called**); the same pair occurs in v. 4 and the noun occurs in 1:18. "Call" language once more reminds the reader of the OT language of election already so evident in 1:3-14. As God previously chose, destined, and appointed Israel, so God has now called, destined, and chosen **you,** the basically Gentile readers, to leave behind former ways of living and live as the chosen people of God. This verse dominates the final three chapters of Ephesians, as aspect after aspect of the Christian's life is viewed from the perspective of the call.

Before these individual aspects are discussed, the author indicates in vv. 2-3 various characteristics of the Christian walk of life. In fact he does not return to the basic exhortation until v. 17. The first characteristic is **lowliness** (v. 2), a term found not only here in Ephesians but also in Acts 20:19; Phil. 2:3; Col. 2:18; 2:23; 3:12—the likely source of our verse; and 1 Peter 5:5.[21] Although **lowliness** does occur in Josephus and Epictetus, it is used there only in a negative sense; it, together with **meekness,** was much more highly evaluated in the OT (Prov. 3:34, for example) and in the Dead Sea Scrolls (1QS 2:24; 4:3; 5:3, 25). Once those virtues or characteristics came to be associated with Jesus, their positive evaluation within the Christian community increased (Matt. 11:29). **Lowliness** is the characteristic of a person who does not insist on his or her rights; **meekness** is the characteristic of the humble person who does not need to serve self first. **Patience** can refer to endurance of suffering, but here it more likely refers to the slowness in avenging a wrong which is called for by **for-bearing one another in love.** That is, mutual patience and mutual bearing of one another's weaknesses are marks in the Christian community of the very love that God has shown (1:4-5; 2:4; 3:18-19).

The Christian ethical walk is further to be carried out by an eagerness **to maintain the unity of the Spirit in the bond of peace** (see Col. 3:14). The Greek words are stronger. "To be **eager**" (*spoudazō*) means to spare no effort or expense; **to maintain** (*tēreō*) is to hold on and preserve something that has already been given, namely, the unity given by the Spirit. The word **unity** occurs only in v. 3 and v. 13 of Ephesians 4; it does not occur elsewhere in the NT, although it is quite common in the letters of Ignatius of Antioch (ca. 110-117). Buried in the word **unity** or "oneness" is the word **one** (*hen*), which is resumed in v. 4 with **one body.** First, however, the author answers the question of *how* unity is to be maintained: **in the bond of peace. Bond** is from the same root word as "prisoner" (v. 1) and it means that which binds together. The bonding agent is **peace,** which in 2:14 has been identified as Christ. How is Christ "our peace"? Above all by uniting Jew and Gentile, a unity expressed in the **one body** of the church (v. 4). Unity, therefore, is not dependent on a fleeting attitude of "hail-fellow-well-met"; unity depends on God's activity in Christ. The implicit judgment on contemporary divisions within the church is clear.

Verse 4, then, begins a discussion of the **body** (of Christ) that continues through v. 16; the section is reminiscent of the discussions in Romans 12 and 1 Corinthians 12. Verses 4-6 have the lyrical quality of a hymn or possibly a confessional formula, particularly when v. 4*b* (**just as . . .**) is identified as an alteration of a pre-Ephesian piece of material.[22] The material could also well be a catechetical formulation, quite possibly connected with Baptism. Verse 4 emphasizes the unity of the church; in doing so it picks up phrases the author has already used. The church is **one body** (2:16; 1:22-23) united by **the Spirit** (4:3; 2:18). Members of the body are **called** in **hope** (1:18), the basis of which is contained in v. 5: **one Lord** (1:2-3, the basic confession of the Hellenistic church; 1 Cor. 12:3), **one faith** (1:13, here with perhaps the sense of "doctrine" or "system of belief"), and **one baptism** (no specific prior verse, but in general the entire preceding work). One wonders whether v. 5 is written to combat specific opponents. Verse 6, in this little hymn on unity, celebrates the oneness of the **God and Father of . . . all,** (RSV's **us** is not in the Greek; for Father see 1:2, 3, 17; 2:18; 3:14; 5:20; 6:23). He is the God **who is above all and through all and in all,** which, in isolation from its context, could easily fit into a pantheistic conception of God. What rescues the words from that interpretation is that this universal statement about God is applied to God's activity for and in the church (see similar material in 1 Cor. 8:6). In addition this verse as well as the previous two provide the motive or reason for the very worldly exhortation of v. 1; once more the author is recalling to his readers the basics of Christianity. Once more, it should also be pointed out, **Spirit, Lord,** and **God/Father** occur in close proximity.

Elaboration on Unity in Terms of Gifts (4:7-16)

Having briefly introduced the theme of the body, the author elaborates on that theme in language strongly reminiscent of Romans 12 and 1 Corinthians 12. The body is one (v. 4), but the individual gifts and abilities of the body members are multifaceted; neither the various gifts nor their bearers are to be homogenized into an undifferentiated mass. Thus the concern of unity and diversity, so important to the primitive as well as the contemporary church, is the subject of the section.

Verse 7 states the basic principle: God gave **grace** to each believer. In 3:2, 7-8 Paul is viewed as a special recipient of God's grace; that thought could easily have developed into a doctrine of a special office for Paul and others. Instead, the author affirms that grace was given to **each of us.**[23] **According to the measure of Christ's gift** can be understood in two ways. Many commentators point to Rom. 8:32 and argue from that verse that, since God did not hold back his Son, so his generosity in giving spiritual gifts through Christ likewise holds nothing back. What seems more likely, given the overall context of the passage, is that each gift given to believers is in fact measured and therefore limited; it is for that very reason that all the gifts are needed for the proper functioning of the body (vv. 11-16). The word **measure** also appears in vv. 13 and 16 (in the latter verse it is buried in the English translation).

The giving of **gifts** is supported by the quotation of Ps. 68:18, which is introduced by **therefore it is said.** The Greek reads "therefore it says," the "it" perhaps referring to Scripture. The quotation is basically from the Septuagint, with one major exception: the psalm reads that he was "receiving gifts among men." In the psalm God is the victor who marches up (to Zion?), trailing his captives behind him and receiving tribute from his enemies. The Ephesian quotation reverses the direction of the last thought; God *gives* gifts, and it is that thought which links vv. 7 and 8 to each other, as well as v. 8 to vv. 11-16. RSV's **he led a host of captives** is weak; literally the phrase reads "he took captive captivity." The author reapplies the quotation. Christ is the victor; he fought a battle on high and captured his enemies (cf. also 6:10-20). Who are the captives? Probably the aeons and powers of the air already mentioned (2:2, 7; 3:9).

Verses 9-10 are a little commentary or midrash on the verse. The ascending is interpreted as the heavenly ascent of the resurrected Jesus; such an ascent demands a prior descent and, in harmony with the Christ hymn of Phil. 2:5-11, that descent is understood as the incarnation of Christ. Some have understood the descent **into the lower parts of the earth** as a descent into Hades or Sheol, where Christ proclaimed the gospel to the dead (cf. 1 Peter 3:19). **The lower parts of the earth,** however, in Gnostic thought would refer to this physical earth (see NEB and Phillips); in ascending, the redeemer figure passes through the various heavens, triumphing as he goes until he reaches the highest heaven, which is **far above all the heavens** (cf. Heb. 4:14; 7:26; John 6:33, 38, 41-42, 50-51, 58, 62; 3:13-15). It is possible that by stressing that the same person both **descended** and **ascended** the author is combatting the heresy which denied a full incarnation of Christ in the man Jesus. The positive result of the ascent is that Christ is now able to **fill all things** (see 1:23). Ascension does not mean God-abandonment but a Christ-filled world (cf. TEV on v. 10). He can distribute **his gifts** everywhere, and so v. 11 returns to the matter of gifts, detailing some of them (see v. 7).

The gifts are people who serve various functions within the body. **Apostles** and **prophets** have already been mentioned in 2:20 and 3:5; they are the original recipients of the revelation. **Evangelists** are mentioned elsewhere only in Acts 21:8 and 2 Tim. 4:5; the term likely refers to wandering preachers of the gospel, whereas **pastors and teachers** (probably, according to the Greek grammatical construction, to be understood as one group) are more settled in their ministries, serving one congregation or one small group of congregations. **Pastors,** a translation of the Greek word for shepherds, is not used elsewhere in the Pauline materials (the verbal form occurs in Acts 20:28). **Teacher** occurs in Rom. 2:20; 1 Cor. 12:28-29; 1 Tim. 2:7; 2 Tim. 1:11; 4:3.

More important than the designations are the functions of these gifts of Christ. Their activity is **to equip the saints for the work of ministry, for building up the body of Christ.** In Greek the different prepositions used to introduce each clause indicate that **to equip the saints** is the main thought, with the other two phrases subordinate to it. "Equipping" was used in politics for bringing together people of different factions so that the work of government could continue. The saints are thus to be equipped by the ministers **for the work of ministry,** which belongs to all of God's people (**saints**). The result is that the body of Christ is strengthened. There are horizons to this activity, which at the same time are its goals (v. 13): **unity of the faith** and unity **of the knowledge of the Son of God** (see 4:3,5; 1:15,17; 2:8; 3:12,17,19; 6:16-23) as well as **mature manhood** and **the measure of the stature of the fulness of Christ. We all** is emphasized; the perspective is communal rather than individualistic, even when the thought reaches **mature manhood,** which literally is "to a perfect man," possibly referring to the new man of 2:15 (contrast Col. 1:28).[24] **The measure** (cf. v. 7) is **the fulness of Christ,** that is, the maturity (rather than **stature**) shown by Christ and given by him. Christ is thus the measure of true mature humanity.

The opposite is continued existence as immature children (v. 14; see 1 Cor. 14:20) who are tossed around like a rudderless boat or who are so lightweight in their thinking that they are blown around by **every** gust of **wind** that brings with it some new teaching. **Cunning** refers to a dice game in which one person cheats another. **Deceitful wiles** refers to an encouragement to someone to wander from the truth.

Is the author directly confronting opponents who are active in the recipient congregation? Quite likely, especially when the clustering of Gnostic terminology is recognized: **ascend, descend, fill, fulness,** and **perfect man.** Once opponents are identified, the ministry of the leaders and of all the saints is seen to be even more crucial, in part because they guarantee the tradition. The answer to immaturity, division, and heresy is the same answer given in 1 Corinthians: **love.** The author thus outlines the task of every Christian: to speak **the truth in love,** not to ride roughshod over another person nor to sacrifice the truth for the sake of harmony, but to speak the truth in a way sensitive to the needs and limitations of the listeners. The result is the very growth in Christian maturity spoken of in v. 13. The body, on the one hand, is to grow into **the head, Christ** (v. 15; see also 5:23; 1:22; Col. 1:18; 2:10); on the other hand, it is from that very head that the body is united in such a way that it is able to grow (v. 16; see Col. 2:19). Verse 16 resumes language previously utilized: **the whole body** picks up vv. 4 and 12; **joined together** repeats a word used in 2:21 and recalls the motif of the church as a holy temple; **when each part is working properly** contains the word "working," used in 1:19 and 3:7, and "measure," used in 4:7 and 13; **upbuilds itself** repeats 2:21 and 4:12; and **in love** resumes not only 4:15 but also numerous other passages (1:14, 15; 2:4; 3:18-19; 4:2, 15).

Three matters are especially clear: First, the verbs are present tense; the activity of growth is ongoing, not complete. Second, each part is needed for the proper functioning of the body, but at the same time it is the growth of the whole that is emphasized. Third, the basis of the growth is love.

Having elaborated on the unity of the body of Christ, the author next returns to the theme of ethics already announced in v. 1.

Return to Basic Exhortation (4:17—6:20)

Negative Exhortation (4:17-19)

The author resumes the exhortation of v. 1 (**no longer live as the Gentiles do** is literally "no longer walk as the Gentiles walk"). Just as v. 1 began with the solemn designation of Paul as "a prisoner for the Lord," so v. 17 begins with what is almost an oath, **I affirm and testify in the Lord.** Christians are no longer to walk as Gentiles; one could almost translate the term as "pagans." And how do they walk? **In the futility of their minds,** that is, in the emptiness of their minds and lives, which have no real content (cf. Rom. 1:21). The futility is expressed in two ways: **they are darkened in their understanding,** which means that they have no insight into the great plan of God which has been the theme of Ephesians, as opposed to the apostle's prayer for the readers (1:18); and they are **alienated from the life of God,** which recalls us to the parallel thought of 2:12. **The life of God** is the life of which God is the author, and it is that life which is so unknown to the Gentiles apart from Christ that they are dead (2:1-5). The reason for their alienation is also twofold: they are ignorant (of God), an **ignorance** which in the NT is virtually synonymous with sin; and they have hard hearts, which is a frequent biblical image. **Hardness** means a loss of feeling; the Gentiles are so hardened, so petrified that they have no power to feel at all. They are calloused (both **hardness** and **callous** are medical terms) and have therefore handed themselves over to the control of immoral behavior (v. 19; Rom. 1:18-32 develops more fully the same basic thoughts).

Positive Exhortation Based on Baptism (4:20-24)

Verse 20 begins with what in Greek is an emphatic contrast to the preceding verse: but **you did not so learn Christ.** "Learning Christ" means not only an intellectual or emotional response to Christ; it also includes one's ethical walk of life. The verb **learn** has as a derivative the term "disciple"; to **learn Christ** thus affects how one lives. The contrast between **you** and nonbelievers is followed in v. 21 by a brief aside quite similar to 3:2. The readers are reminded that truth, as opposed to the ignorance of the Gentiles (v. 18), is present in Jesus. Verses 20-21 thus recall the basic baptismal teaching received by the readers.

Verses 22-24 contain three closely related imperatives. The first command is to **put off** the old man, or possibly the old humanity. RSV's **nature** is quite misleading, for the Greek term is *anthrōpos* ("man"). The old man is passé; he belongs to a former existence which is being destroyed by the very desires to which he is devoted. A radical change is demanded; not only do old habits need to be corrected, but the whole individual needs to be changed. That change, that putting off, is similar to the parallel thought of Rom. 6:6, where Paul talks of an actual death in Baptism of the old man. We will return to possible baptismal connections, but it is of note that in the pillar epistles the new existence is conceived as a future covering rather than a present-tense taking off of the old man (see especially 2 Cor. 5:4). Paul does, however, speak of putting off "the works of darkness" in Rom. 13:12, and elsewhere too "putting off" has a strong ethical connotation (Eph. 4:25; Col. 3:8; Heb. 12:1; James 1:21; 1 Peter 2:1). Whereas the tense of the first command implies a single action, the present tense of the second command (v. 23) indicates a continuing, repeated action (cf. 2 Cor. 4:16). The renewal is of **the spirit of your minds. Spirit** is the essence of a person, what makes her or him "tick." That the mind is being renewed harks back to v. 17 (see also Rom. 12:2). The believer is being changed in such a way that he or she is new, indeed a new creation (2 Cor. 5:17 and Eph. 2:15). This continuing process is well expressed by Luther as a daily return to Baptism. The legitimacy of a baptismal reference is supported by the third command, which once more indicates a single action: **put on.** In the early church, in which immersion of adults was the norm, individuals to be baptized took off their old clothes and donned white robes symbolizing the putting on of Christ. We see such references in Rom. 13:14 and Gal. 3:27. The "new man" of Eph. 4:24 may thus have a double reference to both Christ as new man/humanity and the Christian as part of that new humanity created through Baptism. This new man is **created after the likeness of God,** that is, it is created according to the will of God.[25] The characteristics of this baptized new humanity are **righteousness and holiness.**

The Christian, says the author of Ephesians, lives in an unchristian world and therefore the Christian by his or her life is to be sharply distinguished from the world. The danger for the recipients was, in a sense, a loss of memory, for they stood in danger of forgetting who they were. The result of forgetting would be a reassimilation to the way of life they had left, *unless* they, in light of their Baptism, were continually renewed.

Implications (4:25—5:2)

Exhortation One: Truthfulness (4:25).   The section that begins in 4:25 and ends in 5:2 is a series of loosely joined exhortations that brings out the implications of putting off the old humanity. As did the apostle Paul before him, so also the author of Ephesians utilizes ethical directions which in many cases are identical with the best non-Christian moral advice of the day; the specifically Christian element is the motivation the author develops for the various directives. The author may also be using catechetical materials designed for adult instruction which outlined what the new Christian had to renounce. **Therefore** links v. 25 with what has immediately preceded it, and **putting away** repeats the verb used in v. 22 and translated there as "put off." **Falsehood** or lying is suggested by the word "true" in v. 24. The actual command comes in the form of an OT quotation from Zech. 8:16; the quotation is modified by its Ephesian context: in v. 21 we are told that "the truth is in Jesus" and in v. 15 we have already learned that growing into the head means "speaking the truth in love." **Truth,** then, is the Christian message applied to human relationships, as is evident in the positive reason given for the command, **for we are members one of another.** That reason harks back to vv. 15-16 (see also 5:30) and recalls the image of the church as the body of Christ.

Exhortation Two: Sinless Anger (4:26-27).   Once more the command is in the form of an OT quotation, in this case, Ps. 4:5 (4:4 in RSV): **be angry but do not sin.** The command, despite the opinion of many commentators, says nothing about righteous anger but rather addresses the ease with which anger passes over to sin. Actually, the Hebrew verbal form lying behind the Greek has more the sense, "*if* you are angry do not sin" (cf. NEB and TEV), which is a step removed from Col. 3:8, where anger per se is simply prohibited. The basic command is supported by two other commands. The first directs that anger be brief; the second directs that Christian life be lived in such a way that **the devil** would have **no opportunity.** The Greek reads, "give no place to the devil," that is, give him no opening, no entree, no room to operate. **Devil** occurs again in 6:11; the term is not used in the pillar epistles of Paul (see Introduction, n. 2).

Exhortation Three: Stealing (4:28).   The third exhortation has the same pattern as the first: negative command, positive command, reason. The former thief is to work **with his hands** (see also 1 Thess. 4:11), which may reflect the positive attitude toward manual work evidenced by Paul (Acts 18:3; 1 Cor. 4:12; cf. 2 Thess. 3:8; the attitude goes back to Pharisaic Judaism). What is of real interest is the motivation for the commands: the ability to help others (see also Titus 3:14; James 2:14-17; 1 John 3:17). The goal of work is not acquisition but contribution.

Exhortation Four: Speech (4:29).   This exhortation somewhat follows the pattern of exhortations one and three. The prohibition is against **evil talk**. **Evil** translates a word that means diseased or rotten; "foul" talk might be closer to the original. The positive command is to utilize speech **for edifying**, that is, building up others (*oikodomē*). The term has already been used in 2:21; 4:12; and 4:16, in each case for the upbuilding of the body, which is the church. Here, in this last occurrence of the term in Ephesians, it is used for the very practical matter of how we use our gift of speech; the theme will reappear in 5:4 (see also Matt. 15:11, 18; 12:34; James 3:6-12). The reason for the command is to encourage the readers to speak in ways that **impart grace to those who hear**. **Grace** has been used repeatedly in Ephesians to characterize God's activity; Christians take part in that activity by proper use of their words in teaching, preaching, and conversation. The Ephesian concept is expressed by Luther's idea of the mutual consolation of the brethren, upbuilding dialog between believers.

Exhortation Five: Ethic concerning the Spirit (4:30).   Since the Holy Spirit is the basic gift given by God to his people and since that gift is to direct and control everything the Christian does, failure to live as God's new people **grieves the Spirit**. **The Spirit** is further defined in relationship to Baptism: **in whom you were sealed for the day of redemption**. The phrase refers to 1:13-14 and thus helps to unite the two halves of the letter. "Sealing" is a reference to Baptism and alludes, in part, to the protective function of the seal that was placed on a document or box. In the Spirit the Christian is safeguarded **for the day of redemption**. In 1:7 the author wrote, "we have redemption." In 1:14, where "redemption" is hidden in the English translation, redemption is future. **Redemption**, therefore, is both present and future in Ephesians. In 4:30 the reference is also future, to the day of the Lord, the coming of Christ (1 Thess. 5:2; 1 Cor. 1:8; 2 Cor. 1:14; 2 Thess. 2:2).

Exhortation Six: Behavior in the Community (4:31-32). Negative command, positive command, and reason once again provide the structure. A laundry list of vices is mentioned, all of which are summarized in the term **malice. Let . . . be put away** may be a divine passive, in which case the readers are directed to allow God to work in them. The positive command briefly outlines how the new person is to act. Of special significance is the concern for life in community: **be kind**[26] **to** *one another,* . . . **forgiving** *one another.* The reason for such behavior is that God has already forgiven them (see the parallel in Col. 3:12-13). Once more the author bases his imperatives on the indicative of what God has done. How can the Christian refuse to forgive when God has forgiven her or him? (Cf. the Lord's Prayer.)

Exhortation Seven: Summary (5:1-2). Verse 1 makes explicit what was implicit in 4:32, namely, that the Christian is to imitate **God.** Eph. 5:1 is the only explicit directive in the entire Bible that calls the community to imitate God. The Paul of the undisputed letters calls on his readers to imitate him and through him to imitate Christ (1 Cor. 11:1; 4:16-17; 1 Thess. 1:6; Phil. 3:17) and he can speak directly of imitating Christ (Phil. 2:5), but he never speaks in this straightforward way of imitating God. Behind the command is the Ephesian view of God as Father, since the readers are to imitate God **as beloved children** imitate their parents. Further, the recipients are to **walk in love. Walk** picks up the same terminology used in 4:1 and 17, and one wonders if the implicit reference to God as Father is carried over to the language of v. 2; after all, how does a child learn to walk? From its parents. The children are **beloved** and they are to walk **in love,** another common Ephesian theme. The Christian ethic is a love ethic. The reason for such an ethic is the twofold activity of **Christ,** who **loved us and gave himself up for us** (also 5:25 and Gal. 2:20) as a sacrifice to God. To walk in love, therefore, is how the Christian imitates God.

Exhortations on Negative Behavior (5:3-20)
Negative Exhortation (5:3-4). Having paused for a brief, albeit important statement of how Christians are positively to respond to God's love in Christ, the author returns in 5:3 to the

listing of prohibitions begun already in 4:17. The three specific activities prohibited are **fornication and all impurity or covetousness.** While most commentators see specific references here to sexual misconduct, the terms need not be limited in meaning to that one form of behavior. The same three terms occur in the solemn teaching in v. 5. In Judaism these sins are particularly identified as Gentile or pagan sins (cf. 4:17-19). These sins are so serious they should not even be mentioned, **as is fitting among saints.** Strong parallels with the Dead Sea Scrolls are evident here: the people of Qumran are also to be separated from those around them and, even more significantly, the three sins mentioned in Eph. 5:3 are, in a sense, the cardinal sins in the thinking of the community of the Scrolls (CD 4:15-18). Anything impure which would defile that priestly community is to be avoided. Whatever his exact relationship with Qumran, the author utilizes the thought of the Jewish sectarians to express his ethics, as he does throughout this section (vv. 3-20). Verse 4 in Greek continues the sentence begun in v. 3. Various misuses of speech are mentioned as also being unfitting; the word translated **levity** means ill humor or dirty stories, and not simply the joviality which RSV's **levity** indicates. What is to be substituted for that misuse of language is **thanksgiving** (cf. 1QS 9:26—10:6). The term does not imply the Lord's Supper (that use is found only in a variant reading at 1 Cor. 10:16), but probably does indicate prayer, as is supported by v. 20, where the verbal form occurs.

Solemn Teaching (5:5). The author introduces this sentence with a solemn command: **Be sure of this.** "Be absolutely certain!" The triad of vices from v. 3 is resumed at a personal level, with the additional further specification of the covetous person as an idolater. None of those listed has the inheritance which is promised to the saints (1:14 and 18). The inheritance which will be denied is that which is **in the kingdom of Christ and of God. Kingdom** is not a common word in the Pauline literature; in fact, most scholars feel it is taken from pre-Pauline church tradition. The Ephesian occurrence is unique in that it is the only time in the NT that **kingdom of Christ** is used (2 Peter 1:11 and Rev. 11:15 have "kingdom of our Lord"). The ethical response expected of Christians is thus given an eschatological (end-time) motivation, as is found also in 1 Cor. 6:9-10 and Gal. 5:19-21, where the same catechetical tradition is found.

Warning (5:6).   Is there another hint here of false teaching (see also 4:14)? Perhaps. The content of the deception is **empty words,** which may well indicate that false teachers are suggesting the types of immoral behavior condemned in vv. 3-5. Such deception is dangerous, for the immorality it counsels causes **the wrath of God** to come **upon the sons of disobedience. The wrath of God** is God's eschatological (final) judgment, which is already being worked out in the world (Rom. 1:18). **Sons of disobedience,** found in the NT only here, in 2:2, and in a disputed reading at Col. 3:6, is once again a term which may come from the Dead Sea Scrolls (cf. "sons of perversity," "sons of darkness," and "sons of destruction").

Command Based on Warning (5:7-14).   The command issued in vv. 7 and 11 is an implication of the warning found in v. 6. Christians are to separate themselves from immoral companions (cf. the Dead Sea Scrolls and 2 Cor. 6:14—7:1, which has often been identified as a non-Pauline fragment).[27] The reason for such separation is given in v. 8: **For once you** [Gentiles] **were darkness, but now you are light in the Lord.** Their former status was **darkness,** their present status is **light. Light** is frequently used as a symbol for God (1 John 1:5, for example) and thus also for Jesus (John 8:12; 9:1-41), and by extension walking in the light means living a Christian, as opposed to a pagan, life (Rom. 13:12-13; John 12:35-36). The recipients have been converted and have passed from darkness to light (see also Acts 26:18; Col. 1:13; and 1 Peter 2:9); they are, therefore, to **walk as children of light,** which reiterates directives already announced in 4:1 and 5:2. The light/darkness dichotomy also occurs at Qumran (1QS 3:18-21), although it seems to be utilized to some extent as a baptismal reference in early Christianity (1 Peter 2:9; Heb. 6:4; and the present section). Verse 9 briefly outlines the products of the light; the triad listed here may be constructed in conscious opposition to the earlier triads of vices (vv. 3, 4, and 5; see 1QS 2:24-25). RSV makes v. 10 into an independent command parallel to v. 8*c*; in content v. 10 is really a modifier that indicates *how* Christians are to **walk as children of light,** namely, by seeking **what is pleasing to the Lord.** No Christian law exists for every situation and therefore Christians must diligently seek God's will (cf. Rom. 12:2).

Verse 11 resumes the prohibition of v. 7, although this time also picking up from v. 9 the criterion of **fruits.** Instead of participating in the unfruitfulness of darkness, Christians are to **expose** it (implicitly, by means of the light). The reasons for such activity are outlined in vv. 12-14: what is done by the sons of disobedience should not even be mentioned (cf. v. 3), but exposure of the sin reveals it and may lead the sinner to make the same move from darkness to light already made by the Christian (cf. 1 Cor. 14:24-25; Matt. 18:15; John 3:20-21). That interpretation is supported by the hymn quoted in v. 14, which may well be a baptismal hymn. While of unknown origin (perhaps taken from Gnosticism), the hymn is somewhat parallel to Rom. 6:4 in its emphasis on a death in Baptism; more clearly parallel is Eph. 2:5-6, where death, life, and resurrection also occur in a passage that we have already argued is baptismal. The one who sleeps is dead in trespasses (cf. 1 Thess. 5:7); **light** is a symbol of the salvation God gives and to which the recipients are called once again in this writing which is an extended reminder of Baptism.

Resumption of Command (5:15-17).   Verse 15 resumes the command of v. 8, which in turn repeats 5:1-2; 4:17; and 4:1. The wise person walks in such a way that he or she makes **the most of the time,** since **the days are evil** (cf. 6:13; Gal. 1:4; Rom. 12:2). The command is restated negatively in v. 17*a*, which resumes the wise/foolish distinction of v. 15; v. 17*b* repeats v. 10 and in its emphasis on **understanding** also harks back to the **wise** of v.

15. God's will was an early theme in the letter (1:1,5,9,11; 3:11); it is resumed here and in 6:6. That repetition in chaps. 4–6 of themes stated in chaps. 1–3 is a device by which the two halves of the letter are joined together.

Command concerning the Spirit (5:18-20).   The pattern so common in 4:25ff. of giving a negative command followed by a positive command is evident in v. 18. The Christian, in a sense, is to be **drunk**—not with wine but **with the Spirit,** as the believer is to **be filled with the Spirit. Filled** and "fulness" are by now old Ephesian friends, having appeared previously in 1:10,23; 3:19; 4:10,13. The contrast drawn here may be between the wine-induced frenzies popular in a number of pagan cults such as the cult of Dionysus and the Spirit-induced ecstasy of Christianity which results in **psalms and hymns and spiritual songs** (see Col. 3:16, where the word of Christ is the agent). The goal of the Christian life is thus viewed as a constant state of thanksgiving (see v. 4, as well as Col. 3:17 and 1 Thess. 5:18), in which Christians give thanks in the name of the Lord Jesus Christ.[28]

Exhortations on Subjection (5:21—6:9)

Fundamental Principle (5:21).   Verse 21 introduces the so-called *Haustafeln*, or table of household duties, in which various relationships within the extended family or household are clarified from a Christological perspective (similar "tables" are found in Col. 3:18—4:1; 1 Tim. 6:1-10; Titus 2:1-10; 1 Peter 2:13—3:9; all show the influence of Hellenistic popular philosophy as mediated through Hellenistic Judaism). This initial verse also states the principle that dominates the entire section: mutual subjection of Christians to each other **out of reverence for Christ. Reverence** should perhaps be translated "fear" (as it is in 6:5), namely, the holy fear that people should have before Christ (cf. Ps. 34:9; Prov. 3:7; etc.) The principle of mutual subjection is evident throughout the Pauline literature, as the Christian is called to servanthood and concern for the other (Gal. 5:13; 1 Cor. 8:1-13;

11:17-33; 12:1—14:33a; Rom. 14:1-23). The submission or subjection is a mutual yielding in love, as the believer voluntarily
gives up his or her own wishes for the sake of others. Compare
Luther's words in *The Freedom of a Christian:* "A Christian is a
perfectly free lord of all, subject to none. A Christian is a perfectly
dutiful servant of all, subject to all."[29] The Ephesian *Haustafel*
is the only such NT list to begin with this call to mutual subjection,
which already qualifies the patriarchal nature of what follows.
The qualification is especially noted when our passage is compared with Col. 3:18, where only wives are to be subject.

Subjection within Marriage (5:22-33).   The concept of mutual
subjection is first of all applied to marriage. In Greek **be subject**
does not occur in v. 22 but is implicitly carried over from v. 21,
which is actually part of the same sentence as vv. 22-24. The
relationship of wives and husbands is thus seen clearly in light
of the *mutual* subjection of v. 21. The motivation is crucial: **as to
the Lord,** that is, Jesus. The same motivation is listed for the
child-parent and slave-master relationships. The motivation is
extended in a comparison of the husband-wife relationship and
the Christ-church relationship (vv. 23-24):

    a. **The husband** (masculine noun) **is the head of the wife** (fem-
        inine noun) *as*

    b. **Christ** (masculine noun) **is the head of the church** (feminine
        noun)

    but **as**

    b.[1] **the church is subject to Christ,** thus also

    a.[1] **wives** are **subject to their husbands.**

The chiastic structure (*abba*) is interesting in and of itself, but
it serves to emphasize the importance of the comparisons—and
also the way in which the comparisons qualify the subjection.
Without doubt the author adopts the standard view of his day,
that the husband is dominant over his wife; **the husband is the
head** (see 1 Cor. 11:3). But in Ephesians does that imply blind
power for the husband? In 1:22-23 Christ is the head of all things
for the sake of the church; in 4:15-16 Christ is the head from

whom the whole body grows and upbuilds itself in love. "Headship" thus implies an other-directedness that results in growth and love, rather than a "headship" that means brute dominance. That judgment is confirmed by v. 23b, which somewhat breaks the parallel structure: **. . . his body, and is himself its Savior.** That is, Christ as the head saves, which includes not only redemption but also protection and preservation.[30]

Within the overall context of male domination, the qualification of the power of the husband is continued in vv. 25ff., as husbands are addressed. They are directed to love their wives, and once more a Christological comparison is made. The husbands are to **love** (*agapaō*) **as Christ loved** (*agapaō*) **the church and gave himself up for her.** Verse 25 repeats the language already encountered in 5:1-2; "to give up" (*paradidōmi*) is an early Christian term for the self-sacrifice of Christ (e.g., Rom. 4:25; 8:32; 1 Cor. 11:23; Gal. 2:20; Mark 9:31; 10:33), which is further underlined by the preposition **for,** or "on behalf of" (*hyper*). The verb **love** refers to God's self-giving activity in Christ. Thus the husband is urged to take Christ's love for the church as the pattern of his attitude toward his wife; self-sacrifice, not dominance, is the pattern (also in vv. 28 and 33).

In vv. 25b-27 the author uses language from the marriage customs of the day to explain why Christ died for the church (some identify here a pre-Pauline hymn). First, a dowry needed to be paid for the bride; second, the bride needed to be washed in a prenuptial bath; third, the bride was presented in virginal purity to her groom. Christ is the active agent at each step. He pays the price for the bride, the church (v. 25b). Further, he makes holy his impure bride ("sanctifies her") **having cleansed her by the washing of water with the word. Having cleansed** refers to a completed past action, likely Baptism. That reference is confirmed by the rest of the verse, which views Baptism as a cleansing bath that uses water and the word as agents. In Pauline literature **word** (*rhēma*) is always used for the word of God (see especially Rom. 10:8, 17), and it occurs again in 6:17 with reference to "the sword of the Spirit, which is the word of God." The phrase in v. 26 may refer to the formula of Baptism.

In v. 27 the analogy begins to break down as Christ functions as both the father of the bride (the presenter) and the bridegroom (cf. Col. 1:22; 2 Cor. 4:14; 11:2). The church is to be presented **in splendor** (*endoksos*), a derivative of "glory" (*doksa*), which has been so prominent in Ephesians (1:6,12,14,17,18; 3:13,16,21). The indications of the church's splendor are that she is to be **without spot or wrinkle . . . , that she might be holy and without blemish.** But this is nothing new in Ephesians; see already 1:4, where "we" have been chosen so "that we should be holy and blameless before him." Christ thus fulfills each of the steps leading to marriage; once more the initiative is all on his side, not the church's. Elsewhere, too, the church is the bride of Christ (2 Cor. 11:2; Rev. 21:2; 22:17), an image that may be built on the OT image of Israel as the bride of God (Ezek. 16:1-14 and Song of Songs; others see a reference to the Gnostic image of Christ and the church as a syzygy).

Having somewhat digressed, the author in v. 28 returns to the issue of husbands and wives. **Even so:** that is, even as Christ has shown his love for the church, so **husbands should love their wives.** The verb **should** indicates a moral obligation; the love is not optional. The reason given for such love at first glance seems very self-serving, however: by loving his wife the husband is really loving himself (vv. 28*b*-30). The perspective is somewhat higher, though, than enlightened self-interest. One key to the section is contained in v. 29, where the author turns from referring to "bodies" to writing of **flesh.** Why? Probably the author is anticipating the Genesis quotation in v. 31 which includes the phrase **one flesh.** The second key is the sheer usage of *agapaō* for **love,** since the term indicates self-sacrifice. The third key is the understanding of the church as the body of Christ; as Christ loves his body, the church, so in the analogy is the husband to love his body, his wife. For those reasons the husband and Christ nourish and cherish their bodies (v. 29). "Nourish" is especially used for rearing children; "cherish" carries the sense of making warm. Both terms, therefore, are rather intimate and point to the unity of husband/wife and Christ/church which is the issue in vv. 28-32. The author in v. 30 shifts person and reminds his readers that they, too, are involved in this discussion, **because** *we* **are members of his body.**

The biblical or historical basis for the argument is contained in v. 31 in the LXX quotation of Gen. 2:24 (also quoted in Matt. 19:5; Mark 10:6; and, in a different context, 1 Cor. 6:16). The emphasis in the verse is on the **one flesh,** the unity effected in marriage. It is the same theme of unity that dominates the author's interpretation of the quotation (v. 32). The **mystery,** the author acknowledges, is a great one; he thus uses **mystery** in a way quite similar to the use in the Dead Sea Scrolls, in which frequently a text is quoted, a mystery is said to exist in the text, and the text is then interpreted. The author is careful to indicate that the interpretation is his own (**I am saying that it refers to**), but he is still bold enough to take the rather straightforward statement about marriage and apply it to the relationship of Christ and the church. Thus this **mystery** is given a Christological focus, as are the other mysteries in Ephesians (1:9; 3:3, 4, 9; 6:19). The author may also be countering the peculiar use of the Genesis passage by Gnostics, for whom sexual reunion implied salvation and presexual unity, or he may be countering those who devalued marriage and sexual relations. As if to counter a preoccupation with such heavenly speculations the author rather abruptly returns to earth in v. 33 with a summary statement that once more addresses husbands in terms of love and wives in terms of submission. He individualizes his exhortation: not to husbands and wives (plural) does he speak but to **each one of you** and **the wife.**

The author of Ephesians thus adopts, likely via Colossians, the standard patriarchal view of marriage current in his society. Yet he sharply expands and modifies the brief directives of Col. 3:18-19 by emphasizing the analogy between Christ/church and husband/wife in terms of love. While he uses the occasion of speaking of marriage eloquently to explore the relationship of Christ and church, he also uses this relationship as a prototype of what marriage is to be. He thus uses the great mystery to provide the pattern for the mundane relationships of marriage.

Subjection within the Family (6:1-9). The exhortations on subjection move in 6:1-9 to other relationships within the structure of the family: children and parents (6:1-4) and slaves and masters (6:5-9). A common pattern of development is evident:
- addressees,
- imperative verb,
- recipient of the action,
- mode or reason for the action.

What is also structurally evident is that the directions to the subordinate persons (children and slaves) are more extensively developed than the directions to the superior individuals (fathers and masters). At the same time each relationship is viewed from a Christological perspective, much as was the marriage relationship in 5:22-23, and a specifically Christian motivation is given for each action. The cosmic Christ is thus related to the everyday realities of human existence.

As in 5:22 the subordinates are addressed first: children are to **obey.** The Greek word for **obey** carries the sense of "listen to and heed" (*hypakouō*). The children are to obey their **parents** (not only their fathers) **in the Lord.** That is, it is because of their relationship with the Lord Jesus that children are to obey.[31] A second reason is also given: **this is right** (*dikaion*, "righteous"), a reason that could be affirmed not only by the biblical tradition but by the Graeco-Roman as well. In vv. 2-3 yet a third reason is given, namely, a biblical basis from the Ten Commandments. The quotation, essentially taken from the LXX, is divided into two parts, apparently to emphasize the promise in v. 3. The RSV properly translates **earth** rather than the "land" of Exod. 20:12, for the concern is no longer that of the promised land but life anywhere on the earth. Many scholars find it odd that Paul would be concerned with a long life in this world, since he expected the world to end momentarily, and so they see in vv. 2 and 3 another bit of evidence pointing to authorship by someone other than the historical Paul.

It is of note that children are specifically addressed, especially when we recall the letter's salutation: "To the saints who are also faithful in Christ Jesus" (1:1). Children quite clearly were considered part of the Christian community. Verse 4 contains a briefer exhortation, although it is still complete. Only the fathers are addressed (it is possible but not probable that mothers are included), and they are given a double command: negatively, not to **provoke** their **children to anger,** and positively, to **bring them up in the discipline and instruction of the Lord. Instruction** is the milder of the two nouns and refers to verbal training which could mean scolding or encouraging. **Discipline** is the stricter term and refers to adherence to the rules of the household. It occurs nowhere in the undisputed letters and this Hellenistic ethical term is found in the NT only in later books (2 Tim. 3:16; Heb. 12:5,7,8,11). Both terms are modified by **the Lord.** Lest we understand the father as only a strict disciplinarian, we should note that **bring up** is the same Greek word used in 5:29 and translated there as "nourish."

The third pair of relationships is dealt with in vv. 5-9. As with the children of v. 1, so too the slaves are told to obey (v. 5). The obedience has some interesting qualifications attached to it. It is directed toward **those who are your earthly masters,** literally, "lords according to the flesh." Throughout the section the author utilizes a wordplay that is reflected only in v. 9 of the RSV. The Greek term *kyrios* means both "lord" in the sense of an earthly master or ruler and "Lord" in the sense of the heavenly Lord Jesus. The slave thus serves not only an earthly lord but a heavenly Lord as well (vv. 7-8). The obedience, secondly, is to be carried out **with fear and trembling,** a phrase found in the undisputed letters in 1 Cor. 2:3; 2 Cor. 7:15; and Phil. 2:12 (see also the "fear" in the Greek of Eph. 5:21 and 33 [RSV: "reverence" and "respect"]). The phrase connotes wholesome fear and respect rather than neurotic anxiety (cf. Ps. 2:11; Gen. 9:2). The obedience is also, thirdly, to be done **in singleness of heart; singleness** indicates honesty, single-mindedness, and pure motivation. And finally, the slaves' obedience is to be done **as to Christ.**

Once more the Christological motivation is stated. That motivation is rather fully developed in vv. 6-8. Negatively, the slave is not to serve with the eye, working only when the earthly lord can see and reward (**eyeservice** occurs only here and in Col. 3:22). Positively, the slave is to understand herself or himself as a slave of Christ, whose service is in the final analysis directed not to the earthly lord but to the Lord (v. 7: cf. Paul as a prisoner of Christ in 3:1 and Paul as a slave of Christ in Rom. 1:1; Gal. 1:10; Phil. 1:1). It is not without importance that the slaves are to do the will of God (vv. 6-7); God's will, as we have seen, is a major concern of our author (1:1,5,9,11; 3:11; 5:17). Once more the cosmic (God's will) is to be reflected in the mundane (the behavior of slaves). For that matter, the slave knows that he or she as well as the earthly lord lives in light of the coming judgment (v. 8) when all people will have returned to them the good they have done. Verse 8*b*, "whether he is a slave or free," also indicates the ultimate insignificance of one's earthly social status.

That ultimate insignificance is stated quite boldly in v. 9. The earthly lords (**masters**) are to do the same for the slaves; that is, the masters are to do good to the slaves. Negatively, they are to avoid threatening them. Both actions are rooted in the same Christological basis as the entire paraenetical (hortatory) section. First, the earthly lords are reminded that they also have a Lord and that that same heavenly Lord is the lord of the slaves. Secondly, just as the slaves were reminded of the future judgment so are the lords: **there is no partiality with him. Partiality** literally means "to receive the face," that is, to judge on the basis of external factors such as socioeconomic position (also used of God or Christ in Acts 10:34; Rom. 2:11; Col. 3:25; 1 Peter 1:17). Thus both the slave and the master are in subjection and both will appear before the same judge. Their relative positions are also changed in Christ: the master's position of superiority is qualified since he too has a master; the slave's position of inferiority is qualified since he or she is "freed" from the earthly master in order to serve the heavenly (cf. 1 Cor. 7:17-24). Thus in the last of the three pairs the author, rather obviously dependent throughout on Col. 3:18—4:1, continues to build on and to deepen the tables of household duties he inherited. No area of human relationships was separated from a Christological focus that called for mutuality and respect within the community of Christ.

Concluding Exhortations and Appeal to Emotions (6:10-20)

Exhortation One: Be Strong (6:10).   In 6:10-20 the author finally brings to a conclusion the exhortative section begun already in 4:1. In doing so he or she also all but concludes the letter; only vv. 21-24 remain. We have identified the genre of Ephesians as that of epideictic literature (see the Introduction). According to Aristotle the final section, or epilog, ". . . is composed of four parts: to dispose the hearer favorably towards oneself and unfavorably towards the adversary; to amplify and depreciate; to excite the emotions of the hearer; to recapitulate" (*Ars Rhetorica* 3.19.1). The implicit countering of opposition (rather than an obvious theological locking-of-horns with the foes) causes the author to soften the first two aspects. The third goal of the epilog, however, is clearly present in 6:10-20, as the author dramatically pictures the Christian in mortal combat with the devil. The emotional pitch is increased as each portion of the Christian's spiritual armor is named and then taken up. Such appeals to **be strong, to stand,** and to **pray** are not rare in Paul (Rom. 13:11-14; 1 Cor. 15:58; 16:13; 1 Thess. 5:6, 16-22, 25; cf. Col. 4:2-4), but they are much more extensive here. This section also, though in rather subtle ways, resumes themes from earlier in the letter; in particular we will see how themes from the opening chapter are restated. Such a device, namely, a repetition at the end of themes originally stated at the beginning, is also typical of this kind of literature. The section also arouses pity for the author (v. 20, **ambassador in chains**).

The first of this final series of exhortations is introduced with **finally,** as the author indicates that he is drawing things to a close. The RSV is a bit misleading in translating the next word as **be strong.** In English that phrase carries the sense of self-effort. "Shape up! Be strong!" In Greek, though, the verb is passive: "*Be* strengthened." How? **In the Lord and in the strength of his might.** That is, it is the Lord who strengthens Christian believers, not we who strengthen ourselves. This initial exhortation picks up earlier themes. In 3:16 the author prays that the Father ". . . may grant you to be strengthened with might through his spirit. . . ." Moreover, the phrase from 6:10, **strength of his might,** in Greek is the same phrase as "great might" (RSV) in 1:19. In other words, 6:10 repeats a theme from 1:19. For that matter, **in the Lord** is simply another way of expressing "in Christ" or "in him," which occurs throughout the initial chapter and indeed throughout the entire letter. How does the strengthening occur? God gives his armor.

Exhortation Two: Put On (6:11-12).   **Put on** is found in one other place in Ephesians, at 4:24 ("put on the new nature"), where it occurs immediately after "put off"; the last-related directive, though, was the "putting away" of 4:25. Finally in 6:11 we get the positive counterpart, in which the readers are directed to **put on the whole armor of God. Whole armor** is the correct meaning of the Greek term; the reference is to the entire equipment worn by the heavily armed soldier. This armor is **of God,** which is to be understood as a subjective genitive; that is, the armor belongs to God and is given by him to the believers. That judgment is confirmed by the passages in the OT in which God is viewed as a warrior (Exod. 15:3; Isa. 42:13; 59:15-17; Pss. 7:10-13; 35:1-6; Zech. 14:3; Wis. 5:16-23). That God is the source of the armor is also supported by the immediately preceding verse in Ephesians, in which strength is a divine gift. See also NEB, which translates "the armor which God provides" (similar wording in TEV).

The purpose of wearing the armor is to **be able to stand against the wiles of the devil.** To **be able** is a cognate of "be strong" in v. 10. The ability or strength that is anticipated is the ability to stand, to hold one's position, to keep from yielding (cf. Aboth 5:4; for more on "stand," see the comments on v. 13). The threat to that ability to stand comes from **the devil** and his **wiles. Devil** has occurred already in 4:27, where the readers are advised to "give no opportunity to the devil." **Wiles** has been used in 4:14, where it is used of human deceivers; TEV suggests "evil tricks" as a helpful translation. Our present verse indicates that the misleading strategies are not merely those of people but ultimately stem from the devil himself.

Verse 12 states that thought explicitly. **Contending** translates a noun that means hand-to-hand combat or even wrestling. The fight is an active one for Christians and not one they merely observe. The fight, negatively defined, is not against **flesh and blood** (a common Hebrew expression for humanity; the Greek has "blood and flesh," which also occurs in Heb. 2:14). Indeed, the battle is a cosmic battle **against the principalities, against the powers, against the world rulers of this present darkness, against the spiritual hosts of wickedness in the heavenly places.** We encounter among these foes several familiar concepts. **Principalities** and **powers** are mentioned in 1:21; 2:2; and 3:10; **darkness** occurs at 5:8 and 11; **spiritual** is found in 1:3 and 5:19, although with a positive reference; and **heavenly places** has been used at 1:3; 1:20; 2:6; and 3:10. Only **world rulers** is a new concept. We have already seen in the earlier discussions the quite probable source in Gnosticism for such heavenly beings; **world rulers** would fit the same pattern. The term refers to spirits that have parts of the world under their control. More significant than source is meaning: the battle is with the very heavenly powers that oppose God. One should not, therefore, be naive about the power of evil in the world or in one's own life.

Exhortation Three: Take (6:13).   **Therefore** is a resumptive conjunction in this case; that is, it indicates that the author is resuming the exhortation of vv. 10 and 11 and thus **the whole armor of God** and **stand** are repeated. The number of military terms begins to increase in this verse. **Take,** in its Greek form, is a technical military term for putting on one's heavy armor immediately before the battle. The goal of being armed is **to withstand** (cf. "stand" in v. 11) **in the evil day.** The **evil day** would be a day of special temptation; it may also quite likely indicate the eschatological battle at the end of time and perhaps the day of the Lord as well (see 1 Cor. 1:8; 5:5; 2 Cor. 3:14; Phil. 1:6; 1:10; 2:16; 1 Thess. 5:2-4; Amos 5:18-20). It is not, however, solely to be interpreted as future, for "the days are evil" (5:16); that reference is clearly to the present. The battle is present tense (6:12) and it extends into the future.[32] How the Christian stands now, however, determines how she or he will finally stand. The days are evil now (5:16) and the battle, fought in daily ethical decisions, is being fought now (6:12), not just at the end of time.

The readers are told **to stand, having done all.** The latter term is another military term and has the sense of having carried out one's assignment. And when one has done that he or she stands. **Stand** is an important theological term in Paul's letters. The Christian stands in grace (Rom. 5:2), faith (Rom. 11:20; 2 Cor. 1:24), and the gospel (1 Cor. 15:1). The Lord Jesus makes the believer stand (Rom. 14:4) and those who think that they stand for other reasons should take heed lest they fall (1 Cor. 10:12; see also Col. 4:12). The standing in Ephesians may have a double reference. More literally it may simply refer to surviving the battle, to being able to stand when the conflict is ended. It may also, though, refer to the ability of the armored ones to stand before God on the final day, clad in the very armor God has provided. (One might wonder: is that armor given in Baptism?) The armor is detailed in the following verses.

Exhortation Four: Stand (6:14-16).   The fourth and fifth exhortations tell us *how* the Christian is to stand: namely, by wearing the armor. The verses are out of chronological sequence, in a sense. The actions of vv. 14-17 actually precede the standing; note the aorist participles in vv. 14-16. Thus vv. 14-17 are a commentary or fuller explication of what it means to "take the whole armor of God" and thus of how one does in fact stand (v. 13). The author utilizes the familiar picture from the ancient world of the typical outfit of the Roman soldier.

The Christian first **girds** his or her waist or **loins with truth.** The "girdle" was a broad belt of leather, metal, or cloth and metal together which not only provided support for the soldier but also gave him a place to attach other pieces of equipment. The girdle encircles the soldier in the same way that truth encircles the believer (earlier uses of truth: 1:13; 4:21, 24, 25; 5:19). The **breast-plate,** which protected the throat, heart, and lungs, is a **breast-plate of righteousness** (4:24; 5:9). Both pieces of the soldier's outfit mentioned in v. 14 are in Isaiah connected with the same theological concepts mentioned in Ephesians. In Isa. 11:4-5 the messianic figure is girded with righteousness and truth; in 59:17 the Lord himself puts on "righteousness as a breastplate" (see also Wis. 5:18). The vocabulary used in the LXX and here in Ephesians is virtually identical. In 1 Thess. 5:8, however, the breastplate is viewed as faith and love.

Verse 15 describes the sandals worn by the soldier; made of leather and bound by thongs which were wrapped around the instep and ankle, the sandals worn by a soldier at times had nails driven into them so that they functioned like cleated shoes. A soldier who wore the proper foot equipment was harder to move and could therefore stand well. The paradox is that these sandals of warfare are **equipment of the gospel of peace. Peace** has already occurred in 1:2; 2:14, 15, 17; 4:3; 6:23; **gospel** has been used in 3:6 and 1:13, so that once more we are drawn to the initial chapter of Ephesians. The cleated sandals (boots are also a possibility) are what root the Christian soldier. **Peace** is used of Jesus in 2:14; he is in fact called simply "our peace." Does the author want us to understand Jesus as our rootage, as that which makes us stand? Perhaps. One is also again reminded of Isaiah: "How beautiful upon the mountains are the feet of him who brings good tidings [literally in the LXX, 'preaches the gospel'], who publishes [literally in the LXX, 'preaches the gospel'] peace" (52:7). Thus **gospel** and **peace** are found together in the LXX of Isaiah (cf. Rom. 10:15).

The final piece of equipment mentioned in this exhortation is the **shield of faith** (v. 16). It is introduced with the qualification **besides all these. Faith,** which is mentioned throughout the letter (1:15; 2:8; 3:12, 17; 4:5, 13; 6:23; "you have believed" is also in the important initial blessing, 1:13), is the chief defensive weapon; it is possible that the term here may refer to God's faithfulness (Barth). There is no OT passage closely related to this image, but it does pick up the military art of the time. The shield was a large, door-shaped piece of wood (sometimes two layers of wood) which was covered with canvas and then hide. At the last minute before battle the shield was dipped in water. When **flaming darts,** that is, arrows dipped in pitch and set on fire, hit a shield they simply fizzled out. The image is thus a powerful one. Faith douses **all** the arrows **of the evil one,** the devil (**evil one** is used of the devil only here and in 2 Thess. 3:3; it is not used in this way in the undisputed letters). The Greek word for **evil** (*ponēros*) occurs in a related form in v. 12 ("the spiritual hosts of *wickedness*"). The Christian, therefore, engages in the cosmic battle by means of faith.

Exhortation Five: Take (6:17).   The author introduces a new verb, "receive," which is more closely descriptive of how the soldier dressed than is RSV's **take.** The last two items, the **helmet** and the **sword,** can only be received; the attendant puts on the helmet and hands the soldier his sword. The helmet was made of skin reinforced with metal; the sword was most likely thought of as the short and straight sword of the Roman soldier. The **helmet of salvation** once more takes us to Isa. 59:17 (cf. 1 Thess. 5:8, where it is the hope of salvation that is the helmet). The close relationship of God and salvation is indicated elsewhere in the OT, where God *is* salvation (Pss. 18:2, 46; 35:3; Isa. 33:2; Jer. 3:23). The last item mentioned, the sword, is the only offensive weapon listed. It is a **sword of the Spirit** (Spirit occurs in 1:13, 17; 2:2, 18, 22; 3:5, 16; 4:3, 4, 23, 30; 5:18; 6:18), that is, a sword given by the Spirit. The sword is further styled as **the word of God** (cf. earlier in the paraenetic section, 5:26; also Heb. 4:12). While OT parallels are not quite so obvious, there may be an echo here of Isa. 49:2 (cf. 11:4; Hos. 6:5; 2 Thess. 2:8; and Rev. 19:11-16). There is possibly also a reminiscence of Eph. 1:13 ("you . . . have heard the word of truth"), although a different term for **word** is used there. It is the speaking of the word which reaches out and attacks the enemy (cf. *LBW* 228, stanza 3: ". . . one little word subdues him.")[33]

Exhortation Six: Pray (6:18a). The exhortation to pray may seem oddly placed in this military section, but the components of the armor are not "normal" either! Actually, prayer may be seen as the way in which the Christian appropriates the armor given by God. The constancy in prayer that is demanded is outlined in the next exhortation.

Exhortation Seven: Keep Alert (6:18b-20). The advice is given: **keep alert!** How is that to be done? Through a supplication that is pointed in two directions: for the saints and for Paul. While the specific supplication for the saints is not detailed (but see 1:15 ff. and 3:14 ff.) that for Paul is well developed. The basic request is for a word or **utterance** (*logos*, see 1:13) that will be given to him so that he might open his mouth and with confidence openly make known (RSV's **proclaim** is very misleading) **the mystery of the gospel.** "To make known" **the mystery of the gospel** clearly recalls 1:9, "he has made known to us . . . the mystery of his will." Once again, as if we needed any more evidence, the final exhortative section is linked with the opening blessing. The author's relationship to the gospel is quite simple: he is in chains for it (see 3:1 and 4:1). Yet there is more, for even in his chains, he is **an ambassador** for it (see 2 Cor. 5:20). So he concludes his request for prayer with the hope that he will indeed speak **boldly,** as an ambassador should. Thus, just as chaps. 1 and 3, so also the exhortative section concludes with a request for prayer (see the parallel in Col. 4:2-4).

Christ has won the crucial battle (1:20-23; 4:8-9), but the war goes on. Christians are actively and daily involved in the war but they do not provide their own weapons, whether defensive or offensive. God provides them, though, in a way that is quite similar to other Ephesian discussions of God's power and might. The war is waged with prayer and word, as well as with everyday ethical response. Thus this final dramatic set of exhortations pulls together the entire letter, as has been shown in the case of individual words. The movement of Ephesians has been from glory and praise in chap. 1 to the struggle of chap. 6, but there is a circular as well as a linear direction, since it is in the very struggle that the Christian glorifies God.

Certainly the military language reminds one of similar language in the Dead Sea Scrolls, especially in "The War Scroll," where the OT holy-war imagery is used to picture the end-time battle between the holy ones of Israel and the host of Satan. There are at the same time significant differences. Does Ephesians picture an actual holy war as does Qumran? It seems rather that the weapons of Ephesians are allegorical, designed for a battle between humanity and **the spiritual hosts of wickedness,** whereas in the Dead Sea Scrolls human armies will fight actual battles against human armies (with angelic hosts on each side). It does not seem, moreover, that the military language of the Dead Sea Scrolls occurs in a hortatory context. Yet the use of apocalyptic, military imagery at the least argues for a common background or tradition, which may in fact be found in the final day language of the OT and Jewish apocalyptic literature and in the military language which we have found especially in Isaiah. For that matter, there may have been an early Christian tradition of such military language which was adopted by Ephesians (see Rom. 13:12; 2 Cor. 10:3-6; 1 Thess. 5:8-10).

■ Conclusion (6:21-24)

Commendation of Tychicus (6:21-22)

Verses 21 and 22 are almost a verbatim copy of Col. 4:7-8 (or vice versa, but see the Introduction). Only slight changes distinguish the two commendations. The secondary nature of Eph. 6:21-22 is indicated by the switch in number, from **how I am and what I am doing** (v. 21) to **how we are** (v. 22). In Colossians that switch makes sense, since Timothy is a cosender (1:1) and the author names additional co-workers (4:10-17). In Ephesians, though, Paul is the only sender and no co-workers are named besides **Tychicus.** The one change from Colossians to Ephesians that is worthy of note is that Ephesians omits "fellow servant" as a designation of Tychicus; Paul in Ephesians has no such fellow laborers who are ranked with him. **Tychicus,** who probably is to be understood as the bearer of the letter, is to supplement the letter with an oral report about Paul's condition. According to Acts 20:4, Tychicus was from the province of Asia and accompanied Paul on his final journey to Jerusalem. He is designated by the Paul of Ephesians with the lofty titles of **beloved brother and faithful minister in the Lord.** He is also called a **minister** (*diakonos*) in 2 Tim. 4:12 and Titus 3:12. The further knowledge about Paul and Tychicus' own ministry will comfort the Ephesians.

Benediction (6:23-24)

As is common in Pauline letters, a benediction and wish for peace conclude the document. What is somewhat unusual is that the **peace** is mentioned before **grace;** normally the reverse is true, as in Eph. 1:2. What is also unusual is that the benediction is in the third person rather than the second person (see Rom. 15:33; 1 Cor. 16:23-24; Gal. 6:18; Phil. 4:21-23). The result is that the benediction has a general nature, which fits the rest of the letter quite well. Not only are the recipients wished peace and grace, they are also blessed with **love** and **faith. Love,** a consistent theme of Ephesians, is repeated in the final verse, **grace be with all who love our Lord Jesus Christ.** The RSV translation which ends the letter, **with love undying,** is an extremely free rendering of the Greek, which says simply, "in incorruptibility," or "in immortality." The RSV rendering emphasizes humanity's response; the more likely emphasis is that "in incorruptibility" modifies the word **grace.** It is God's grace that cannot be destroyed, for it is a grace which in love has elected, redeemed, made known the mystery, and which destines these **who love our Lord Jesus Christ** to receive the inheritance, ". . . to the praise of his glory" (1:3-14). Thus the letter, an extended reminder of the implications of Baptism, comes full circle as the prominent themes of peace, love, faith, and grace are once more sounded in the intricate fugue called Ephesians.

NOTES

Introduction

1. Nils A. Dahl, "Ephesians, Letter to the," *IDBS* (1976) 268.

2. That is, letters whose authorship by Paul is not disputed; usually included are Romans, Galatians, 1 and 2 Corinthians, Philippians, 1 Thessalonians, and Philemon. They are also called the pillar epistles.

3. Erwin Nestle and Kurt Aland, eds., *Novum Testamentum Graece,* 25th ed. (Stuttgart: Württembergische Bibelanstalt, 1963). The 26th edition introduces a period after v. 19, but without any manuscript support (Kurt Aland, Matthew Black, Carlo M. Martini, Bruce M. Metzger, and Allen Wikgren, eds., *Novum Testamentum Graece,* 26th ed. [Stuttgart: Deutsche Bibelstiftung, 1979]).

4. Once more the 26th edition inserts periods after vv. 6 and 10. Ernst Käsemann, reflecting earlier comments by Eduard Norden, has this to say about 1:3-14: ". . . the pathetic style of 1:3-14 could be called the most monstrous sentence-conglomeration in the Greek language" ("Epheserbrief," in *Die Religion in Geschichte und Gegenwart,* 3rd ed. [1958] 2:519).

5. As William Sanday and Arthur C. Headlam wrote in their commentary on *The Epistle to the Romans* (The International Critical Commentary; Edinburgh: T. & T. Clark, 1895; 5th ed., 1902; reprinted, 1971) lv: "But in the matter of style it must be confessed that Col. and Eph.—and more especially Eph.—stand at the furthest possible remove from Romans. We may take Eph. and Rom. as marking the extreme poles of difference within the epistles claimed for St. Paul. . . . The language [of Romans] is rapid, terse, incisive; the argument is conducted by a quick cut and thrust of dialectic; . . . [In Ephesians] the rapid argumentative cut and thrust is gone. In its place we have a slowly moving onwards-advancing mass, like a glacier working its way inch by inch down the valley."

6. For more examples see C. Leslie Mitton, *Ephesians* (New Century Bible; Greenwood: Attic, 1976) 11-12.

7. The dependence seems too extensive to be simply a reliance by both Colossians and Ephesians on a common theological tradition.

8. See John Reumann's commentary, p. 109 below.

9. For a convenient chart of further examples see George Johnson, "Ephesians, Letter to the," *IDB* (1962) 2:110-11.

10. Ephesians and 1 Peter, in particular, exhibit strong similarities which may well arise from a common dependence on the same tradition.

11. See especially Andrew T. Lincoln, "The Use of the OT in Ephesians," *Journal for the Study of the New Testament* 14 (1982) 44-50.

12. Ernst Käsemann, "Das Interpretationsproblem des Epheserbriefes," in his *Exegetische Versuche and Besinnungen*, 2nd ed. (Göttingen: Vandenhoeck & Ruprecht, 1965) 2:253-61; "Ephesians and Acts," in *Studies in Luke-Acts* (ed. Leander E. Keck and J. Louis Martyn; Nashville/New York: Abingdon, 1966) 288-97; "Paul and Early Catholicism," in his *New Testament Questions of Today* (Philadelphia: Fortress, 1969) 235-51; *Jesus Means Freedom* (Philadelphia: Fortress, 1970) 88-93.

13. Klaus Koch, "Pseudonymous Writing," *IDBS* (1976) 712-14.

14. Edgar J. Goodspeed, *The Meaning of Ephesians* (Chicago: University of Chicago, 1933); *The Key to Ephesians* (Chicago: University of Chicago, 1956).

15. John C. Kirby, *Ephesians: Baptism and Pentecost. An Inquiry into the Structure and Purpose of the Epistle to the Ephesians* (London: SPCK, 1968).

16. Ralph P. Martin, "An Epistle in Search of a Life-Setting," *Expository Times* 79 (1968) 296-302.

17. Nils A. Dahl, "Anamnesis," *Studia Theologica* 1 (1947 [1948]) 69-95 (see also the somewhat abbreviated English version in *Jesus in the Memory of the Early Church: Essays by Nils Alstrup Dahl* [Minneapolis: Augsburg, 1976] 11-29); "Adresse und Proömium des Epheserbriefes," *Theologische Zeitschrift* 7 (1951) 241-64; *A Short Commentary on the Epistle to the Ephesians* (New Haven: privately printed, 1966); "Ephesians, Letter to the," *IDBS* (1976) 268-79; "Interpreting Ephesians: Then and Now," *Currents in Theology and Mission* 5 (1978) 133-43 (also in *Theology Digest* 25 [1977] 305-15).

18. Dahl, *IDBS*, 268.

19. Major discussions from antiquity are found in Aristotle, *Ars Rhetorica* 1.3; 1.9; 3.16-17; Quintilian, *Institutio Oratoria* 3.7; and Menander, *Peri epideiktikōn*. The first two are available in English translation in the Loeb Classical Library series. Menander is available in D. A.

Russell and N. G. Wilson, eds., *Menander Rhetor* (Oxford: Clarendon, 1981). The basic scholarly study is Theodore C. Burgess, *Epideictic Literature* (Chicago: University of Chicago, 1902).

20. On categories see Burgess, ibid., 110-12, 186-87.
21. Ephesians was a favorite book of second-century Gnostics; see Elaine Pagels, *The Gnostic Paul: Gnostic Exegesis of the Pauline Letters* (Philadelphia: Fortress, 1975) 115-33.

Commentary

1. On the phrase "at Ephesus" see above, p. 18 of Introduction.
2. Cf. NEB, "believers incorporate in Christ Jesus"; TEV, "who are faithful in their life in union with Christ Jesus."
3. Eph. 1:3-14 and 1 Peter 1:3-12 are quite close in structure and content; both may have roots in baptismal liturgy.
4. There is also a high probability that the author of Ephesians is basing his thoughts on Col. 1:3-23. See Jack T. Sanders, "Hymnic Elements in Ephesians 1–3," *Zeitschrift für die neutestamentliche Wissenschaft* 56 (1965) 227-29.
5. Another wordplay is buried in the translation of v. 6. Literally it reads: ". . . his grace with which he en-graced us . . . ."
6. In a strongly attested reading, "the love" is omitted, so that the verse reads: "I have heard of your faith in the Lord Jesus and in all the saints." The reading results in a singular NT reference to faith in the saints. Most text critics express reservations because of the singularity of the reading. In addition, the presence of *tēn* ("the") immediately before and after the noun *agapē* ("love") likely provided the occasion for an early scribe's eye to skip the words.
7. The more usual construction is to believe "into" (*eis*).
8. Quoted in Matt. 22:44; Mark 12:36; Luke 20:42-43; Acts 2:34-35; Heb. 1:13; it is alluded to many other times. Ps. 8:6 seems to be reflected in v. 22.
9. The battle is not completely over, however; see 6:10-17.
10. Mitton (65-66) includes a chart on the Colossian parallels to the thanksgiving section.
11. Ernest Best, "Dead in Trespasses and Sins (Eph. 2.1)," *Journal for the Study of the New Testament* 13 (1981) 16.
12. Wayne A. Meeks, "In One Body: The Unity of Humankind in Colossians and Ephesians," in *God's Christ and His People: Studies in Honour of Nils Alstrup Dahl*, ed. Jacob Jervell and Wayne A. Meeks (Oslo: Universitetsforlaget, 1977) 213.
13. Cf. Col. 3:10-11. See my dissertation, *The Unity of Mankind in Antiquity and in Paul* (Claremont Graduate School and University

Center; Ann Arbor, Mich.: University Microfilms International, 1981).

14. On Christians as a third race see 1 Cor. 1:22-24; 10:32; Clement, *Stromateis* 3.10.10; 6.5.39-41; *Diognetus* 1; *Apologia Aristidis* 2, 16, 17; Tertullian, *Ad Nationes* 1.8: *Scorpiace* 10.

15. Heinrich Schlier, *Der Brief an die Epheser; ein Kommentar* (5th ed.; Düsseldorf: Patmos, 1965).

16. William J. Brandt, *The Rhetoric of Argumentation* (Indianapolis/New York: Bobbs-Merrill, 1970) 16.

17. M. C. De Boer, "Images of Paul in the Post-Apostolic Period," *Catholic Biblical Quarterly* 42 (1980) 368-69, sees the emphasis on Paul's sufferings as another indication of the post-Pauline nature of Ephesians.

18. M. Barth's translation (*Ephesians* [Anchor Bible 34; Garden City: Doubleday, 1974] 367), "[to grow] toward the Inner Man," i.e., Jesus, is possible only because he "borrows" from other passages (p. 369).

19. W. Foerster, *"aksios, anaksios, aksioō, kataksioō,"* *Theological Dictionary of the New Testament* 1 (1964) 379.

20. TEV translates the passage in a strongly legalistic way: "Live a life that measures up to the standard God set when he called you." Col. 1:10 also has "walk" and "worthy" in the same verse.

21. Related forms of the word occur in Matthew, Luke, Romans, 2 Corinthians, Philippians, James, and 1 Peter.

22. Possibly **one hope** was part of the original first line. It is possible that the original hymn began with v. 6, with vv. 5 and 4 following in that order. The progression would be from the one God to the one Lord, faith, and Baptism, and thence to the one body. The order of the original would have been reversed because of the argument in vv. 1-3. (I am indebted to Roy Harrisville for this insight.)

23. There is a wordplay here that is difficult to reproduce in English. Vv. 4-6 repeatedly use the word "one"; v. 7 begins in Greek: "To one each of us." I.e., the first word in v. 7 is "one" (*heni*), which is to be understood in relationship to all the "ones" of the previous verses.

24. Although the term in 2:15 is *anthrōpos*, "humanity," while the term in 4:13 is *anēr*, "man," "male human being."

25. "Likeness" is carried over by the RSV translators from the word "image," which occurs in Col. 3:10.

26. "Kind" translates *chrēstoi*, which may be a wordplay on *Christō*, "Christ," in the same verse.

27. Joseph A. Fitzmyer, "Qumran and the Interpolated Paragraph in 2 Cor. 6, 14–7, 1," *Catholic Biblical Quarterly* 23 (1961) 271-80; Hans

Dieter Betz, "2 Cor. 6:14—7:1: An Anti-Pauline Fragment?" *Journal of Biblical Literature* 92 (1973) 88-108.

28. A. Campbell King ("Ephesians in the Light of Form Criticism," *Expository Times* 63 [1952] 276) points out that church instruction on worship is often placed after a discussion of renunciation and before a discussion on obedience and subordination, as in Ephesians 4–5; cf. Col. 3:16-17.
29. *Luther's Works* 31:344.
30. In Greek v. 24 begins "but as." The RSV omits the "but," which may be the author's way of indicating that the analogy is not perfect, since the husband does not save his wife or his own body.
31. The textual evidence for and against including **in the Lord** is evenly balanced, but the fact that p⁴⁶, Sinaiticus, and Alexandrinus all include the words is rather strong evidence for their originality.
32. In Gnosticism the battle is between the soul that seeks to ascend and the heavenly powers that try to stop it; cf. v. 12.
33. Actually the entire stanza is reminiscent of Eph. 6:11–17:

> *Though hordes of devils fill the land*
> *All threat'ning to devour us,*
> *We tremble not, unmoved we stand;*
> *They cannot overpow'r us.*
> *This world's prince may rage,*
> *In fierce war engage.*
> *He is doomed to fail;*
> *God's judgment must prevail!*
> *One little word subdues him.*

Note also in stanza 4 the reference to God's battle activity: "For God himself fights by our side/With weapons of the Spirit."

SELECTED BIBLIOGRAPHY

Abbott, Thomas K. *A Critical and Exegetical Commentary on the Epistles to the Ephesians and to the Colossians.* International Critical Commentary. Edinburgh: Clark, 1897; reprint edition, 1956. Obviously seriously out-of-date in terms of discoveries made in the last 80 years (such as the Dead Sea Scrolls), Abbott remains one of the few commentaries that deal seriously with Greek grammatical and philological issues.

Barth, Markus. *Ephesians.* Anchor Bible 34 and 34a. Garden City: Doubleday, 1974. Barth's work is by far the most thorough of the recent commentaries in English. His massive study contains helpful extended discussions of key problems. His approach also provides a balance to the present commentary, particularly regarding questions of authorship and possible Gnostic influence.

Beare, Francis W. "The Epistle to the Ephesians," in *The Interpreter's Bible* 10. Nashville: Abingdon, 1953. Beare's commentary is an older, popular-level study that is still quite instructive.

Caird, G. B. *Paul's Letters from Prison (Ephesians, Philippians, Colossians, Philemon).* New Clarendon Bible. London: Oxford University, 1976. The commentary by Caird is a relatively brief but insightful look at the epistle.

Dahl, Nils A. *A Short Commentary on the Epistle to the Ephesians.* New Haven: n.p., 1966. This short work (50 pages) by Professor Dahl is a downpayment on a larger commentary which is still anticipated. Although he has modified his views on authorship since writing this short study, he has provided a popular-level but deeply theological look at Ephesians.

Houlden, James L. *Paul's Letters from Prison: Philippians, Colossians, Philemon, and Ephesians.* Westminster Pelican Commentaries. Philadelphia: Westminster, 1977. Houlden's commentary is nontechnical but it nevertheless allows insights from the Greek to inform his English exegesis.

Mitton, C. Leslie. *Ephesians.* New Century Bible. Greenwood: Attic, 1976. Mitton, as Houlden, writes a commentary for a general audience which at the same time allows insights from Greek to inform his study. The volume is a helpful introduction to the major issues in the interpretation of Ephesians. It also counters at many points the work of Barth.

Sampley, J. Paul. "The Letter to the Ephesians," in *Ephesians, Colossians, 2 Thessalonians, The Pastoral Epistles.* Proclamation Commentaries; Philadelphia: Fortress, 1978. Sampley provides a top-notch introduction to the critical and theological issues that must be addressed in studying Ephesians. His summaries of the theology of Ephesians are particularly good.

Thompson, G. H. P. *The Letters of Paul to the Ephesians, to the Colossians, and to Philemon.* The Cambridge Bible Commentary on the New English Bible. Cambridge: Cambridge University Press, 1967. Thompson's commentary, based on the NEB text, provides brief comments on significant terms and phrases. He has somewhat less concern for explaining entire sentences or paragraphs.

Four commentaries in German must be mentioned. The first is a ground-breaking work in the history of scholarship on Ephesians; the final three represent the latest in continental scholarship on our epistle. Schnackenburg's work is especially helpful.

Schlier, Heinrich. *Der Brief an die Epheser; ein Kommentar.* 7th ed. Düsseldorf: Patmos, 1971.

Gnilka, Joachim. *Der Epheserbrief.* Herders theologischer Kommentar zum Neuen Testament. Freiburg: Herder, 1971.

Mussner, Franz. *Der Brief an die Epheser.* Oekumenischer Taschenbuchkommentar zum Neuen Testament 10. Gütersloh: Mohn, 1982.

Schnackenburg, Rudolf. *Der Brief an die Epheser.* Evangelisch-Katholischer Kommentar zum Neuen Testament. Neukirchen-Vluyn: Neukirchener Verlag and Zurich/Einsiedeln/Cologne: Benziger Verlag, 1982.

ABOUT THE AUTHOR

Walter F. Taylor Jr. is Associate Professor of New Testament at Trinity Lutheran Seminary in Columbus, Ohio. A native of Omaha, Nebraska, he is a graduate of Midland Lutheran College, The Lutheran Theological Seminary at Philadelphia, and Claremont Graduate School (Ph.D., 1981). He also studied at Yale University Divinity School. From 1973 to 1976 he was Instructor in Greek at the School of Theology at Claremont; from 1978-81 he was Associate Pastor at First Lutheran Church, Lincoln, Nebraska. Dr. Taylor edits the *Trinity Seminary Review* and is a frequent speaker on Paul, Mark, and evangelism at conventions, convocations, and congregations.

COLOSSIANS

John H. P. Reumann

INTRODUCTION TO COLOSSIANS

The Letter to the Colossians, one of the "Prison Letters," has only in recent years come into its own. Addressed by Paul and Timothy (1:1) to a Christian community at Colossae, a town in the Lycus Valley about 100 miles southeast of Ephesus in Asia Minor, this four-chapter document shows us Paul imprisoned (4:3, 18; see also v. 10), though we are not told where. He writes rather personally; the "we" form (1:3, 9, 28) often gives way to statements that begin "I, Paul . . ." (1:23-25, 29; 2:1-5; 4:18). Following the usual structure in his letters, he presents afresh the doctrinal foundations of what God has done for us in the gospel, draws out some pertinent ethical implications, and, in this case, warns polemically against a "philosophy" of false teachers that threatens the gospel at Colossae (see the Outline).

As long as Colossians was viewed within the Pauline corpus as one of the "Prison Letters," it tended to be overshadowed by the longer book of Ephesians (which contains many verbatim phrases from Colossians, though often with considerable expansions), by the more vivid Philippians (likely Paul's last letter), and even the little but very appealing note to Philemon (with which Colossians in chap. 4 shares a list of personal names that is almost totally the same). But once scholarly examination of the Bible began to propose different possible places of origin for the several letters Paul wrote from prison and once critical scholarship raised questions about some of them as possibly deutero-Pauline (that is, not by Paul himself but by members of his "school" of followers), Colossians came to have a more independent role.

One passage has often stood out. The analysis of 1:15-20 as a "Christ hymn," first by Friedrich Schleiermacher as long ago as 1832, focused intense interest on a portion of chap. 1. Dr. Joseph Sittler, in addressing the World Council of Churches Assembly at New Delhi, India, in 1961, used 1:15-20 as an ecumenical "call to unity" that would outflank old disputes over Christology and salvation by appealing to Christ as ruler over "all things" in nature and thus to a "cosmic Christ." In this way he brought Colossians to the forefront of much theological and popular bridge building between church and world in the last two decades. So much, indeed, has the literature on this hymn multiplied that its application in what follows at 1:21ff. and the controversy in chap. 2 (where the true heart of the letter lies) have at times been almost overlooked. Yet so sonorous and majestic is the epistle, though at times quite simple, practical, and down-to-earth, that one can resonate to Adolf Deissmann's comment, "When I open the chapel door of the Epistle to the Colossians, it is to me as if Johann Sebastian [Bach] himself sat at the organ."[1]

Historical circumstances which form the background for Colossians are partly clear, partly uncertain. Paul himself had evidently not yet in his missionary career been at the town of Colossae or its neighbors, Laodicea eight and one-half miles to the west and Hierapolis across the valley (4:13-17; cf. Philemon). Evangelization of the area had instead been carried out by one Epaphras, a Colossian, working on behalf of the Pauline mission (1:7; 4:12-13). But Epaphras encountered difficulties in dealing with a new "philosophy" that talked of "the elemental spirits of the universe" (2:8). Proponents of these ideas implied that the Pauline gospel of "justification by grace through faith" and even the Christ he preached and Paul's notion of "salvation" did not suffice cosmologically (the magic theme to the heretical teachers!) as an interpretation of all that exists in the universe. Epaphras therefore came to Paul for help. Since Paul, in prison, could not go in person, this letter is the response.

The place of Paul's imprisonment when all this happened has traditionally been taken to be Rome, from where Paul wrote about A.D. 60. Such was the opinion of some scribes who appended to Greek manuscripts the note appearing after 4:18 in the KJV, "Written from Rome to Colossae by Tychicus and Onesimus." But beginning in 1799 Caesarea in Palestine—where Paul was imprisoned for some two years, perhaps A.D. 56-58 (Acts 23:23—27:1)—was proposed. Moreover, from 1897 on (though the suggestion had been made in antiquity), Ephesus was endorsed by others. Ephesus, where Paul labored for over two years (ca. A.D. 53-54; see Acts 19:1-21), is in fact even closer to the Lycus Valley and would have been the urban center from which the faith was spread throughout Asia Minor by evangelists like Epaphras.

Scrutiny of the language, style, and contents of Colossians has increasingly in recent years led also to the view that our epistle is the work of someone other than Paul himself, though a disciple of his. It is sometimes argued that even during Paul's lifetime some assistant from his circle of missionary helpers might have been entrusted with drafting a portion of a letter. No doubt after his death these persons, as a "school," kept on expounding Pauline views, but in the face of new situations. If one wishes to hazard a guess, Timothy (1:1) or Epaphras might even have been the individual, the actual author from within the Pauline school, who wrote Colossians. In this case the date of composition could have been anytime from around A.D. 60 till the end of the first century. Details of style and language are not discussed extensively below, but some of the commentaries noted in the Selected Bibliography explore the matter in great detail.[2] Illustrations of possible shifts in doctrinal contents from the views of Paul himself can be seen in the new development of the "body of Christ" figure (see on 1:18; 2:19) and in the eschatology (below, on 3:1-4).

A complicating factor for most views are the ancient references to the apparent destruction of Colossae in an earthquake of A.D. 60-61 and the fact that it was never rebuilt. (Archeological diggings have been planned there in recent times but never carried

out.) Those supporting authorship by Paul should presume a date
before this destruction (thus it militates somewhat against Rome).
Those claiming that Colossians is pseudonymous must recognize
that it would then be an epistle in Paul's name to a place no
longer existing (but linked to the Colossian area by the names
from the letter to Philemon).

Excellent commentaries have been written in the last 30 years
assuming each of these varied theories. One of my teachers, C.
F. D. Moule of Cambridge, argues for Rome about the year 60
with authorship by Paul himself; and another, Eduard Lohse,
then professor at Göttingen, for a document by a Paulinist who
knew the letter to Philemon and who wrote Colossians about A.D.
80 from Ephesus. I have benefited, in preparing these pages,
from the two treatments of Colossians by R. P. Martin (whose
more conservative conclusion is that Paul wrote the letter from
Ephesus during the period described in Acts 19–20); from the
commentary by Eduard Schweizer, in a Protestant-Catholic series, now happily available in English (with Schweizer's thesis
that Colossians is "neither Pauline nor post-Pauline" but by Timothy, on behalf of the imprisoned Paul at Ephesus, about the
same time as Philemon was written); and from the work of a
German Catholic, J. Gnilka (by Timothy, from Ephesus, about
70). My own preference, reflected in this commentary, is for some
follower of Paul, perhaps Timothy himself, in the face of new
needs and questions about "Christ and the cosmos." The date
could be shortly after 70. There is no necessity, if Colossae as a
town no longer existed, to try to pinpoint the menacing "philosophy" there and its false teachers. The opponents depicted may
be a composite. I do not, therefore, in the pages that follow, try
to define who these opponents were; we do not precisely know.[3]
Colossians is, in a sense, a Pauline "catholic epistle," retaining
some specifics from the Lycus Valley but speaking the Pauline
word wherever and whenever someone or something threatens
to usurp Christ's unique role. But my views on the origins of
Colossians, like those of others, are tentative; one dare not be
dogmatic on any theory about the setting of this document. The

late John A. T. Robinson, in a tour de force, argued, as part of his proposal that all New Testament books could have been written before A.D. 70, that Colossians was penned by Paul in the summer of the year 58 while he was imprisoned in Caesarea.[4] Thus the traditional view finds its defenders still today.

In view of such debates and in light of the format and space proportions of the Augsburg Commentary series, I have chosen to concentrate on the text of Colossians itself. A fair amount of Pauline and other references as well as further explanation is presented within parentheses. The reader may skip such parenthetical data in order to follow the flow of the sentences more readily. The overall aim remains to lay bare the flow of the thought of Colossians and to enable the Pauline message to be heard afresh.

In a time like ours when syncretistic versions of Christianity, often with a cosmic flair, beckon alluringly (with talk of "Christ *and* this or that" or the "universal implications" of his lordship), Colossians has a specially pertinent message. What are its theological emphases and its pattern of thought?

One is struck by the way Colossians begins with the *gospel message* (1:5,23,25,28) and *Christ* (1:15-20; 2:9,14-16,19) and then, in light of the *ministry* that spreads this word, the ministry of Paul and others (1:23-25,28; 4:3-4,6), goes on to treat *the church*. This body of Christ is a growing worldwide community in which Paul and the Colossians live and labor for its Head (1:6,18,23,26-29; 2:1-2,6-7). The call to *live in the Lord* what they are in Christ goes out with vigor to the Colossians (2:20—4:3) in matters large and small, in worship and home life, with fellow believers and with "outsiders" (4:5) in a pluralistic society. Like Paul generally, Colossians stresses two sides of Christian experience. On the one hand, Christians are no longer what they were prior to Christ, for redemption has come to them (1:13-14; 2:12; 3:1,10), but it is by faith. On the other hand, perfect fulfillment is not yet attained and the life of God remains hidden even for them (3:3). The "glory" is to come (3:4,24), as is the wrath of God (3:6); hence the admonitions continue. Thus an *eschatology* that stresses present "maturity" (1:28; 4:12) perhaps more than future perfection still calls for an *ethics* with imperatives here and now for those in Christ.

If anyone wishes to say that this sequence is like that of the Augsburg Confession—Christ and gospel (though not, in Colossians, explicitly in terms of "justification"), the ministry, the church, and the new obedience—that simply reflects the Pauline nature of each. More to the point is that Colossians proceeds theologically from gospel foundations to Christian life, with, as required, defense of the faith, interlocking in its sequence doctrine, ethics, and apologetics as a living whole. We continue to need all three aspects of gospel truth in that blending of doxology to God and practical witness in life which makes up Colossians. If Colossians is, as seems apparent, a document that means to enhance the reputation and authority of Paul, it is a Paul who is "minister of the gospel and of the church" (1:23-25), all under and for Christ and the will of God. Paul's advice continues to be, "So live in Christ" (2:6).

The purposes Paul had in writing Colossians are, in any case, clear. Giving thanks for the Colossians' concern for him, he encourages those who hear and read his words to grow in their life in Christ, fending off alien teachings about the world, Christ, worship, and ethics that threaten. In particular he sets forth the person of Jesus Christ, who, though image of God and agent in the creation of all things, died and was raised and reigns as Lord for those now reconciled to God by faith in him.

OUTLINE OF COLOSSIANS

I. The Opening (1:1-8)
    A. Salutation (1:1-2)
    B. Prayer (1:3-8)
II. Foundations (1:9—2:7):
    Grounded in the gospel of the all-encompassing Christ, we live in him, bear fruit, and spread the word of God.
    A. Continuing Petition for the Colossians (1:9-11)
    B. Thanks to God for Redemption in Christ (1:12-14)
    C. The Hymn about Christ (1:15-20)
    D. Divine Reconciliation and the Colossians (1:21-23)
    E. Continuing to Advance the Word of God to the Gentile World (1:24-29)
    F. Paul and the Colossians: Personal Resumé (2:1-7)
III. Polemics (2:8-19):
    Holding to the gospel of the all-sufficient Christ and his cross, we oppose deceitful judgments on our liberty and seek to grow in Christ together.
    A. Christ as Sole and Sufficient Savior (2:8-15)
    B. The Result Is Freedom (2:16-19)
IV. Ethics (2:20—4:6):
    Applying the gospel of Christ and freedom with discipline in life, we pursue the way of the Crucified and Risen One in matters great and small.
    A. If Dead with Christ in Baptism, You Need No Rules to Aid Salvation (2:20-23)

COMMENTARY

■ The Opening (1:1-8)

Salutation (1:1-2)

As in Greek letters of the day (cf. Acts 23:26-30), the sender is mentioned first, here (somewhat unusually, coauthors) **Paul . . . and Timothy.** Then are mentioned the addressees, **to the saints and faithful brethren in Christ at Colossae,** and finally the greeting. Instead of the Greek word "greetings" (Acts 23:26, 15:23; James 1:1), Pauline letters employ a Christianized form of the oriental style of direct address (cf. Dan. 4:1): **Grace to you and peace from God our Father.** God's grace always precedes the peace (*shalom,* well-being, salvation) which believers enjoy **in Christ.** Thus already in vv. 1-2 there is double reference to the central theme of the letter, Christ and the life that comes through Christ. But the blessings in Christ are **from God our Father** (cf. on 1:3), the only salutation in Paul's epistles where the Father is mentioned alone.

Paul needs no further introduction than the frequent designation **an apostle of Christ Jesus by the will of God** (cf. 1 Cor. 1:1; Gal. 1:1; Rom. 1:1). The letter will say much more about his sufferings as minister and missionary (1:24—2:5). Timothy **our brother** is not mentioned again in the letter. Though no apostle like Paul, he may be a real author here (see Introduction). A Christian of Jewish-Gentile background, he was one of Paul's missionary assistants (Acts 16:1-4; 17:14-15; 18:5; 19:22; 20:4), often mentioned in the epistles with some warmth, though he may not have been so effective as was, for example, Titus, another assistant, in Corinth (cf. 1 Thess. 1:1; 3:2,6; 2 Thess. 1:1; 1 Cor. 4:17; 16:10; 2 Cor. 1:19; Phil. 2:19; Rom. 16:21; and 1 and 2 Tim. and Heb. 13:23). Timothy is listed as coauthor of 1-2 Thess., 2 Cor., Phil., and Philemon. Col. 1:1-2 is almost word for word like 2 Cor. 1:1 and is in turn closely echoed by Eph. 1:1 (except for omission of Timothy there). The community at Colossae is described as Christians (**brethren** in the RSV includes women) who are holy and **faithful** or "full of faith" because they are incorporated **in Christ** (cf. 2:6, 11-13, through their Baptism).

Prayer (1:3-8)

Greek letters often went on with a brief prayer of thanksgiving to the god(s), usually just for the good health of the writer and the addressee(s). Pauline letters develop this practice in every case except Galatians and 1-2 Timothy, often with liturgical-sounding language. The prayer of thanksgiving beginning at Col. 1:3 goes on in one long sentence through v. 8. Some would also include vv. 9-11, but the petition there starts afresh as a general statement. Others would add v. 12 and what follows, since it begins with the same verb, "give thanks," as in v. 3. The entire chapter has even been taken as part of the prayer, but that is because of the language of thanksgiving and liturgical phrases which pervade the sections. We may outline the structure of vv. 3-8 as on page 117 and then look at the rich content. Note how phrases balance each other at points; e.g., just **as** and **so** (6*b* and *d*); **heard** and **learned** (5*b*, 7); and **we have heard** and **made known to us** (4*a*, 8). Fruit-bearing and growth (6*c*) provide the central emphasis of the unit.

The intricate structure incorporates the triad **faith, love,** and **hope** (vv. 4-5*a*) as well as a triadic reference to **God the Father, Christ Jesus,** and **the Spirit** (though not without difficulties, as we shall note). The worldwide emphasis of Colossians appears in the phrases **all the saints** (v. 4) and **in the whole world** (v. 6). Three clauses are introduced by the same Greek word rendered above "(just) as," vv. 6b, 6d, 7. The heart of the prayer is the gospel's spread (6c). The gospel, present as it is among the Colossians (6a, 6d), is flanked by references to their having heard it through the missionary Epaphras (5b, 7), who also has made known to Paul and Timothy how the Colossians are progressing in their Christianity (4ab, 8). All of this is under the prayer rubric, **We always thank God . . .** (3a).

We always thank   God, the Father . . . (3a)
  when we pray for you (3b)
    because we have heard of your   faith   in Christ Jesus (4a)
             and . . .   love   . . . for all the saints (4b)
     because of the hope laid up for you in heaven (5a),
    of which (hope) **you have heard before in . . . the gospel**
                                                  (5b)
     which has come to you (6a),
    just **as indeed   in the whole world** (6b)
     it is bearing fruit and growing—   (6c)
    so [literally "just as also"] **among yourselves, from the**
                                    day   (6d)
    you heard and understood the grace   of God   in
                                 truth   (6e)
    just **as you learned it from Epaphras . . .** (7),
    [who] **has made known to us your love in the   Spirit** (8).

We (v. 3) means here Paul and Timothy, but as elsewhere in Paul's letters the plural interchanges with the singular "I" (cf. vv. 23, 24; 2:1-5; and 2 Cor. 1:3-7, 15-17). The word **always** may be taken with **thank** (RSV) or with **pray** (Phillips). **Father** was both an ancient Greek and Old Testament title for God (Jer. 3:4; 31:9; Isa. 63:16), used intimately by Jesus (*Abba*, Mark 14:36) and treasured by early Christians (Rom. 8:15; cf. the Lord's Prayer, "[Our] Father"). Here the reference is specifically to God as

Father of our Lord Jesus Christ, indicating that by the resurrection (Gal. 1:1) God made Jesus Lord (Phil. 2:11). While **Christ** was originally a title ("messiah" or "anointed one" translated into Greek) it frequently functions in Colossians as a proper name for Jesus (see 1:27, 28; 2:2, 5, 6, 8; 3:1; etc., and the discussion of 1:24). **Lord** too occurs as a title (2:6; cf. 1:10; 3:13, 18; 4:1). **Father,** in addition to 1:2 and here, is found in Colossians only at 3:17.

Paul's thanksgiving in prayer rests on what he has heard through Epaphras about the Colossians' responsiveness in two key areas, **faith** and **love** (vv. 4, 8). The first, **your** (pl.) communal **faith,** means acceptance of, trust in, and obedience to God and the gospel; **in Christ Jesus** denotes not merely the object of such faith but the realm of Christianity where such faith lives and moves and has its being. The second is **the love you have** for all fellow Christians, the **love** Colossians show **in the Spirit** (v. 8), through hospitality, kindness, etc. (cf. Gal. 5:6, 13*b*, 22-23; Philemon 5, 22). It is a temptation to take faith and love with **hope** (v. 5) as three "cardinal virtues" (cf. 1 Cor. 13:13; 1 Thess. 1:3; 5:8; and elsewhere). But here in Colossians **hope** is given a special prominence; indeed, it seems to be the source for the practice of love and the persistence of faith; **the hope laid up for you in heaven** is the content of the gospel which the Colossians have heard (5*b*). Future and eschatological, it is hope for which one hopes because it is still hidden (cf. 3:1-4). Paul stresses this hope here not only because the gospel preached to Colossae had stressed it but also because he needs to emphasize the future hope in contrast to misleading teachings current in Colossae (2:8ff.). So also he gives faith prominence (vv. 2, 4), even though he is going to stress Christ and grace (v. 6). Eph. 1:15-16 repeats the thoughts of Col. 1:3-5 but without the reference to hope so prominent here.

The gospel which has come to you (vv. 5-6, literally, "which is present among you") is described as **the word of the truth** (cf. 2 Cor. 6:7 KJV; Gal. 2:5, 14) and further as the **grace of God in truth** (v. 6), i.e., the genuine gospel. Does this collection of phrases mean that what Epaphras had preached in Colossae was under some fire as only a partial form of the good news? **Epaphras** (the name is a short form of "Epaphroditus" but he is not to be confused with the Philippian Christian of that name; Phil. 2:25-30; 4:18) is singled out as **our beloved fellow servant, a faithful** (same adjective as in v. 2, same root as the "faith" of the Colossians, v. 4) **minister of** the **Christ** (v. 7; the article in Greek makes it a title, "the Messiah's minister"). As 4:12-13 (cf. Philemon 23) suggests, Epaphras was a native of Colossae who "worked hard" for those Christians in the Lycus Valley, and who here is legitimized by Paul as serving **on our behalf.** (This is the reading of the best Greek manuscripts, but many ancient versions and church fathers have "on *your* behalf.") Note the verbs: the Colossians **heard, understood,** and **learned** the gospel from Epaphras (vv. 6, 7, plus 5, **heard before**). Some think the conversions at Colossae and **the day you heard** were comparatively recent. But **in the whole world** this gospel movement has for a longer time and in a wider realm been **bearing fruit** and **growing,** just as now it is at Colossae.

On the whole, the opening prayer is quite positive about Colossae, but already there are signs of defending "the gospel according to Epaphras" and the future hope. The term **understood** introduces us to a word that is frequent in Colossians, derived from the root *gnōsis,* "knowledge," here meaning "to know thoroughly." And although with RSV we have taken the last words in v. 8 to refer to the Holy Spirit, and others understand "the love the Spirit has given" (TEV; cf. NEB), the phrase can mean simply "your spiritual love." The fact is that the Spirit plays almost no role in Colossians compared to Pauline epistles generally (cf. 2:5, for Paul's **spirit;** adjective at 1:9 and 3:16).

■ **Foundations (1:9—2:7):**

Grounded in the gospel of the all-encompassing Christ, we live in him, bear fruit, and spread the word of God.

The rest of chap. 1 and all of chap. 2 have sometimes been called the "doctrinal" or "expository" part, in contrast to the "ethical" instruction in chaps. 3–4. Actually a good deal of chap. 2, from v. 8 on, is polemical (note the break in RSV after 2:7), and ethical admonition is already introduced at 1:10, **bearing fruit in every good work,** and 2:6, **live in him,** while a missionary thrust is found in 1:25-29, to **proclaim Christ.** What we really have therefore in 1:9ff. is a review of what **the gospel** (1:5, 23) or **word of God** (1:5, 25) is, restated and developed in its implications, doctrinally *and* ethically. The heart of the statement is a terse credo about Christ (1:15-20). This is surrounded by a liturgical-sounding introduction (1:12-14) and a passage where, from the language of the "Christ hymn" (1:15-20), Paul begins to draw out its meaning for the Colossians (1:21-23), with a first-person concern for mission and Christian advance (1:24—2:5). As the letter thus lays the foundation for all Christianity (note the phrases **built up** and **established in the faith,** 2:7; cf. 1:23, and the "growth language," **rooted,** 2:7; **bearing fruit. . . and increasing,** 1:10), our authors write with one eye on what the Colossians (and we) need to have in mind in order to repulse the "hollow speculations" taken up at 2:8ff., but the other eye on the glorious **mystery** of God's salvation in Christ, now revealed (1:26-27). Hence the presentation is very "doxological": it begins indeed with the language of prayer (1:9-11, following 1:3-8) and closes with the word **thanksgiving** (2:6), with which the formal prayer at 1:3 started and which breaks surface at 1:12 as well, **giving thanks to the Father,** and will reappear at 3:17.

Continuing Petition for the Colossians (1:9-11)

And so (literally, "on account of this also") refers back to the good report about the Colossians' Christianity brought by Epaphras, as does **from the day we heard of it.** Good news as well as bad prompts prayer. The content of what Paul and friends keep asking for their sisters and brothers in Colossae is **that you may be filled with the knowledge of his** (God's) **will . . .** (v. 9), this, in turn, for a moral purpose, **to lead a life worthy of the Lord.**

What kind of life that is we find spelled out in three participles (**bearing fruit, increasing,** being **strengthened**), the first two in reverse order ("chiastic" or X-shaped sequence) in Greek:

in every good work ⟍⟋ **bearing fruit,**
and increasing ⟋⟍ **in the knowledge of God** (v. 10),
being **strengthened with all power, according to his glorious might, for all endurance and patience** . . . (v. 11).

It is God who makes this life possible.

One is struck first by how much the wording of vv. 9-11 echoes 1:3-8—in v. 9: "from the day," cf. v. 6; "we [have] heard," cf. v. 4; "pray," cf. v. 9; "for you," cf. v. 3; "knowledge," cf. v. 6, "understood" (the literal Greek meaning was described above); in v. 10: "bearing fruit and increasing," cf. v. 6 (same Greek, though translated "growing" in RSV); and "knowledge" again. Similarly one notes the frequency of "all" (v. 9; v. 11, twice) and "every" (v. 10) (the word "fully" in v. 10 is from the same Greek term); while this may be reminiscent of the "worldwide" emphasis noted in vv. 4 and 6, here the direction is intensive (magnifying, e.g., the strength from God in v. 11), not extensive in outreach.

The stress in these verses on **knowledge** (vv. 9, 10) and phrases like **in all spiritual wisdom and understanding** have sounded "gnostic" to some commentators, and it has been thought possible that these verses anticipate the section on the false teachers (2:8ff.) by using some of their terminology. Perhaps so, but investigations of materials from Qumran over the last 30 years have turned up many parallels precisely to these details in the Dead Sea scrolls. For example, a phrase in v. 10 when rendered by the KJV "unto all pleasing" suggested conduct ingratiating to other people; Qumran evidence helps verify that it means **fully pleasing to him,** i.e., pleasing to God in every walk of life. God will be the judge of our conduct, not the false teachers (2:15). All this points to the observation that the content of the intercession by Paul and friends is thoroughly Jewish and Old Testament in nature, including reference to "good works" and walking **worthy of the Lord.** It is identification of **the Lord** as

Jesus Christ (1:3; 2:6) that makes it specifically Christian. To speak of **wisdom** as our passage does—in Jewish-Old Testament terms— is scriptural, in contrast to a speculative approach. As so often, Paul's prayer has turned out to be ethical, hortatory, and instructional.

Thanks to God for Redemption in Christ (1:12-14)

The text goes on directly with a participle, **giving thanks to the Father,** loosely attached to **you** in v. 11 (itself the third of three participles in the Greek), going back ultimately to **you** in v. 9. Contrary to this rendering in RSV, it is recognized by many commentators that a new section begins here; the participle is the equivalent of an imperative; and **with joy** in v. 10 goes with this new sentence: "Give thanks with joy to the Father" (cf. TEV). God is then described as the one **who has qualified us** (some manuscripts have, and textual critics prefer, "you") **to share in the inheritance of the saints,** i.e., **in** the **light** (v. 12) and as the one who **has delivered us from the dominion of darkness and transferred us to the kingdom of his beloved Son** (v. 13). What this transfer from one realm to another means is expanded in v. 14 by the words, **in whom** (Christ, the Son) **we have redemption,** and **redemption** is then explained as **the forgiveness of sins.**

God's work of redemption in Christ is described in v. 13 in language of "rescue" that reflects the exodus in the Old Testament (cf. Exod. 14:30; 6:6; Judg. 6:9, 13) and God's intervention generally to deliver his people (cf. Judg. 8:34; Ps. 77:11-15; Luke 1:74). Coupled with v. 11 about God's power to "strengthen according to the might of his glory" (itself a very Semitic expression), we have a definite reminder of "the mighty acts and the mightiest act of God."[5] This time the rescue was not from Egypt to a "promised land" in Palestine, but from our bondage to **darkness** and **sins** into "**the kingdom of** (literally) **the Son** of his love" (another Semitism). While the verb **transferred** might have had special meaning to Jews in Asia Minor whose ancestors had been deported there from Palestine by the Seleucid king Antiochus III more than 200 years before, it more likely evoked for Christians generally a "two-kingdoms" view: one is enslaved to the powers of the world and of this age until liberated by God's action (cf. 2:13,20; Gal. 1:4).

The word **kingdom** (of God) is rare outside the Synoptic gospels. In Paul it is usually a sign of very early, pre-Pauline material (1 Cor. 6:9-10; Gal. 5:21), generally with a future reference (cf. 1 Cor. 15:15 and—the only other Pauline passage about a "kingdom *of Christ*"—15:23-28). Here it seems to refer to no interim kingdom but to a present possession. But the kingdom has been reinterpreted, not as a piece of land at the eastern end of the Mediterranean (thus Paul breaks with Jewish hopes), nor as merely "pie in the sky, by-and-by" (so the passage breaks with apocalypticism), but as **redemption** and **forgiveness,** i.e., the liberty that comes with Baptism into Christ. Cf. for **redemption** 1 Cor. 1:30 and Rom. 8:23; for **forgiveness,** Rom. 3:24-25, a pre-Pauline formula, is as close as we can come, for Paul does not use the phrase, though "forgiveness of sins" was common in early Christian proclamation (e.g., Acts 2:38; 13:38-39; Matt. 26:28).[6] Eph. 1:7 parallels our v. 14.

The **darkness** (v. 13) and **light** (v. 12) contrast should be noted. It is age-old, found in the Bible (Gen. 1:2-5; Isa. 45:7; 26:19; 60:1-3) and in other religions and occurring often in early Christianity (1 Peter 2:9; John 1:9; 8:12; Matt. 4:12-16). The change in dominion here from one to the other stems from God **who has qualified us** (better: has empowered, authorized, or made *you* sufficient) **to share in** (literally, for a portion of) **the inheritance of the saints. . . .** Again the gift seems present, not future, and reflects Old Testament language after the conquest of Palestine (Deut. 10:9; 12:12; Josh. 19:9). The usual rendering, **the inheritance of the saints in light,** is *not* to be taken as if it were "the-saints-in-light," for the final phrase goes with "the inheritance." The usual inclination, to take **the saints** in the same sense as at 1:2, for "Christians," is probably to be rejected too. Attempts to equate these "holy ones" with "the elect," or deceased believers, or Jewish Christians are not convincing. The Qumran evidence tips the sense in favor of "the angels." Then the daring, but typically Semitic, sense would be that God through your Baptism into Christ has entitled you to a share **in** the **light,** i.e., with God who is Light, an inheritance with the angels themselves (cf. also on 2:18 below). This would then be **the hope laid up for you in heaven** (v. 5). The shift from the "you" in the call to give thanks in v. 12 to "us" in v. 13 suggests an earlier source at least behind v. 13 or perhaps several sources in liturgical language, put together here in an ad hoc way to serve as the "introit" leading into the hymn about Christ in vv. 15–20.

With such a hope as v. 12 expresses, coupled with rescue and deliverance into Christ's realm and forgiveness available now (vv. 13-14), who would not give thanks to God **with joy?**

The Hymn about Christ (1:15-20)

Mention of the Son (v. 13) brings us to the heart of the gospel (1:5, 23, 25) which Paul and the Colossians share. While there are many succinct formulations in the New Testament about the work and person of Christ, our letter employs a 112-word statement that is both sublime in itself and the foundation for ensuing sections of Colossians and for Christological discussions in our own day. Few passages have been so intensely analyzed in recent years, and so there is a plethora of opinions on almost every detail. However, the view that we deal here with a hymn that can be isolated within the letter has often resulted in failure to notice how it fits into the flow of Colossians 1–2.

To begin with, virtually everyone senses, even in a prose translation like the RSV, a poetic swing and unusual, solemn, indeed hymnic language in these lines. Some editions of the Greek text print vv. 15-18*a* as poetry; some translations (JB, the French *Traduction Oecuménique,* the German *Gute Nachricht)* print all of vv. 15-20 as poetry. There is a difference of opinion as to whether we have two, three, or more "stanzas." There are several features, however, that combine to make a convincing case that we have here a two-stanza composition, first about Christ and creation (15-18*a*) and then about Christ and redemption (18*b*-20).

Notice, for example, the parallelism of lines, especially **He is the image** (v. 15) and **He is the beginning** (18*b*); also **the first-born of all creation** (15*b*) and **the first-born from the dead** (18*c*). Moreover, each of these opening lines is followed by a clause that begins with the same words (RSV, **for in him,** vv. 16, 19). Compare also "And **he is**" as a parallelism in vv. 17*a* and 18*a*, as well as **and through him** in vv. 16*f* and 20*a*. Among other features notice the use of an opening relative pronoun (literally "who" in Greek).

It will be helpful to print out the total text in poetic lines and then discuss some options and the details of the content. Our assumption is that an earlier hymn, probably of Jewish-Hellenistic-Christian origins, has been used in the letter as a starting point for the discussion that follows. (The term "hymn" was known to the author of Colossians; cf. 3:16. Within the categories of "epideictic" speech known from ancient rhetoric [see Ephesians, pp. 22f.], some scholars use the term "encomium" for such a song. Col. 2:9-15 may also contain elements of the encomium form.) In quoting the lines at 1:15-20, Paul and Timothy are making them their own, even if they interpret some features in their own way.

1. Christ and Creation (vv. 15-18a):

15*ab*	**He is the image of the invisible God, the first-born of all creation,**
16*a*	**for in him all things were created,**
16*b*	**in heaven and on earth,**
16*c*	**visible and invisible,**
16*d*	**whether thrones or dominions**
16*e*	**or principalities or authorities—**
16*f*	**all things were created through him and for him.**
17*a*	**He is before all things,**
17*b*	**and in him all things hold together.**
18*a*	**He is the head of the body, the church.**

2. Christot and Redemption (vv. 18b-20):

18*bc*	**He is the beginning, the first-born from the dead,**
18*d*	**that in everything he might be preeminent,**
19	**for in him all the fulness of God was pleased to dwell,**
20*a*	**and through him to reconcile to himself all things,**
20*b*	**whether on earth or in heaven,**
20*c*	**making peace by the blood of his cross.**

The most obvious parallelism involves vv. 15*ab*, 16*a*, and 16*f* with 18*bc*, 19, and 20*a*, the lines printed closest to the left margin; this even presents a "pattern in prepositions," the sequence **in him, through him,** and **for him** in vv. 16*af* and 19-20*a* (**to himself** in 20 is the same in Greek as **for him**).[7] One may also observe the repetition of **in heaven and/or earth** (16*b*, 20*b*). There is clear emphasis on the word **all** (five times in the first stanza, thrice in the second, counting **everything;** cf. on 1:4, 6, 9, 10, 11 above). By judicious rewriting and omissions some scholars can achieve an *absolute* parallelism in the two stanzas. The words of 16*cde*, 18*d* are frequently regarded as later additions. We shall here claim only the words **the church** at the end of 18*a* and **by the blood of the cross** as definite insertions. Some speak of 17*ab*-18*a* (minus **the church**) as the middle strophe of three or as a "linking triplet" of lines," but that breaks up the **in, through, for** balance. We prefer to admit we do not know the exact parameters of what is being quoted and can allow that the original may not have been absolutely uniform in its stanzas.

The religious and cultural backgrounds of phrases vary. It is in vv. 15-18*a* that nonbiblical allusions from history-of-religions parallels are thickest.[8] Verses 16*f*-17-18*a* (minus "the church") can be read as good Stoicism; indeed, Greek texts, especially from the Orphic religion, spoke of the world as "the body of Zeus." Some have felt that the passage, with references to "the church" and "the cross" removed, could be of non-Christian origins, telling of the "myth of the Gnostic redeemer," about a suprahistorical primal Man who leads the elect to their portion above; this reading has become less and less convincing. Still others have always stressed a biblical and Jewish background. The phrase **image of. . . God** recalls Gen. 1:27. A long stream of Old Testament speculation existed which almost personified Wisdom as "the beginning" of God's work, "the first of his acts of old," who was there beside God "like a master workman" at the creation (Prov. 8:22-31); later writers (Wis. 7:26; 9:4,9; Sir. 1:4; Philo) refer to Wisdom as "image," "word," and even "first-born son." One exegetical tour de force has sought to explain Col. 1:16-18 as rabbinic-like wordplay on the Hebrew term for "beginning" at Gen. 1:1 and Prov. 8:20. Another commentator took "reconcile" in 1:20 of the hymn as starting point and sought to explain the twin poles of creation and reconciliation against the background of the Jewish Day of Atonement ("reconciliation"). Such theories are extreme. The history-of-religions background for vv. 15-20 is varied enough that no one explanation will suffice. The lines must have taken shape among Christians (note **first-born from the dead** as a reference to Jesus' resurrection) in a Jewish, Hellenistic milieu.

Some scholars who believe that Paul wrote Colossians regard the apostle as the author of the hymn as well. Others suggest that Paul or some colleague adapted in vv. 15-17 a song about the cosmic meaning of Wisdom and then appended from a different source a hymn concerning redemption in a reworked form. The dominant view, however, is that a pre-Pauline Christian hymn, like Phil. 2:6-11 and 1 Tim. 3:16, is involved. We agree. Such a hymn would likely have been used in worship, it is said, at ecstatic moments like Baptism (or the Lord's Supper) when faith rhapsodizes about the grandeur of the Savior. But the words would be pertinent at any celebration of Jesus' work and resurrection. Whether Paul's missionary assistant Epaphras had taught the words to the Colossians or they had learned it from other teachers such as those of 2:8ff., we cannot tell. Our authors agree with it enough to employ its "Great Christology"[9] with only a few additions and the interpretation that follows in 21ff.

127

In any case, we have first (vv. 15-18*a*) what is the fullest statement in the New Testament about Christ as mediator of creation (cf. 1 Cor. 8:6; John 1:1-5). Some reference to Jesus, such as "The Son of God be praised" or "We believe in Christ the Lord," may originally have preceded. He is the "image of God the invisible" (literal order; cf. Rom. 1:20); that is, Christ reveals God whom no one can see (Exod. 33:18-23; John 1:18). Contrary to later Arianism[10] which took **the first-born of all creation** to mean that Christ was the first of God's many created beings, 1:15*b* refers to his "primacy over all created things" (NEB). When v. 16 says both at its beginning and end that **all things were created** in Christ (16*f* is more literally, "all things have been and are created" in him), it not only provides a "laundry list" of what "all things" encompasses—**in heaven and on earth, visible and invisible,** plus four examples of "heavenly forces" such as we meet in 1 Cor. 15:24; Rom. 8:38; and in Col. 2:15—but also adds they were made for Christ. He is the goal as well as the origin of creation. That Christ **is before all things** implies his preexistence. That **all things hold together** in Christ assigns him a providental role in creation's continuance (cf. Heb. 1:3). That Christ is **the head of the body,** as we have already noted, would for pagans have a cosmological sense: he governs it and is the answer (this statement of faith says) to the age-old quest for what holds things together. On **the church,** see below.

With the stanza on redemption (vv. 18*b*-20) we are on more familiar gospel ground, with almost no Old Testament backgrounds. The tone is set by **first-born from the dead** (cf. Rev. 1:5; Acts 26:33; and an old Pauline phrase, "first fruits" of the dead, 1 Cor. 15:20,23). This key designation (from which **first-born of all creation** in v. 15 may be formed) helps interpret **the beginning:** it is not a creation term here, but speaks of "new creation," the commencement of the eschatological end-time (which in turn brings to fulfillment God's original beginnings), perhaps even the beginning of a new people. The next line, **that in everything he might be preeminent,** sounds so much like 17*a* that some commentators feel it intrusive or superfluous here. It serves the purpose, however, of saying that Jesus Christ is the crown of the new creation too. The reason is that in Christ **all the fulness [of God] was pleased to dwell.** We bracket **of God** because the words do not occur in the Greek; RSV has imported them under the influence of 2:9. One could render, supplying "God" as subject (as KJV in effect did, in italics): "it pleased *the Father* that in him should all fulness dwell." Or one can take "the fulness" as subject (so RSV), but then the question is whether it has any of the technical sense the word had in later Gnostic systems where "the *plēroma*" (fulness) denoted the upper spiritual world of aeons, close to (but not) God. Possibly the original hymn or at least some of its hearers allowed such overtones. Our letter seems to mean either that "the fulness" is equivalent to God himself or the fulness of grace which makes possible life out of death (cf. John 1:16, and 2:9-10 below). The concern, even in the hymn itself, was not ontological but soteriological, that is, not about "essence" or "being" but about God acting to save. As v. 20 puts it, the purpose of all this was through Christ **to reconcile all things to himself** (i.e., to God; the Greek could also mean "to Christ," as JB and NAB bring out). As at v. 16, there is a phrase clarifying **all things** (neuter, including those "heavenly forces" of v. 16): all **on earth or in heaven.** The closing phrase of the hymn, **making peace** (a rare verb; it suggests the restoration of primeval *shalom* as in Isa. 11:6-9), implies that there had been enmity. The Greek adds, ". . .peace *through him*" (cf. KJV "by him, *I say*"; RSV omits).

It is customary to see worldwide, even cosmic, salvation of **all things** in these verses, and "universal redemption" has been predicated on the basis of them by the church father Origen and others. It is necessary before endorsing any "universalism" here, however, to observe the ways in which our letter to Colossae will interpret the passage.

While our author(s) agree(s) with the portrait of Christ's magnitude and magnificence in this hymn, at least two provisos are introduced into the passage. (1) In v. 18*a* **the church** seems an addition both structurally and in terms of content: the Christian church does not belong with creation but is a result of redemption, after Easter. Paul's regular meaning for "**the body** of Christ" (cf. 1 Cor. 12:12-27; Rom. 12:4-5) is the church, not the world (as in the hymn). So in Colossians the "Greek" sense of the world as the body of the deity, if that is what the hymn had meant, is corrected by addition of the two words, **the church.** This will be picked up in vv. 21-29 on the relation of gospel and church to the world. But in this change the Epistle to the Colossians has also introduced a difference in the Pauline sense for "the body of Christ." Hitherto Christ was identified with the whole body or person, feet, hands, ears, eyes, organs, and "those parts of the body which we think less honorable" (1 Cor. 12:14-25). Now Christ is identified just with the head (18*a*). That shift, caused by use of the hymn, has been marked by some as, not an advance, not retrogression, but simply a change, likely between Paul's own thought and deutero-Pauline theology. (2) While the hymn referred to "**making peace by** him [Christ]," there has been added, using the same preposition, a much more specific reference to the atonement, **by the blood of his cross.** Thus we have a "theology of the cross" (cf. 2:14-15 for further assertion of it). More explanations of this grand Christology of 1:15-20 are found in the following four sections.

Divine Reconciliation and the Colossians (1:21-23)

The application of the Christ hymn will be clearer if one draws lines in a Bible from phrases in 1:15-20 to verses where they are picked up and expounded. Some dozen cases are involved in 1:21—2:15. We shall indicate these by quotation marks around the words involved and by cross-references, noting the new interpretations introduced in 1:21ff. **And "you"** (accusative case, direct object). . .**he has now "reconciled"** (vv. 21-22) is the bold way the application begins. Though translations do not indicate it, a few early manuscripts have "you were reconciled (by God)" in v. 22; then the accusative **and you**. . . would follow right along with **all things** in v. 20 as the object of **to reconcile.** The word order clearly means to make **you** (in Colossae) the object of the divine reconciling action, and in distinguishing the hymn from Pauline commentary we must recognize this link. Following the RSV, however, we nonetheless discover two shifts from what the hymn says. (*a*) There is interest in people (**you**), not in **all things** (cf. also 2:13). The application will be personal, existential, to human lives, not cosmological—the "heavenly forces" will in 2:15 be vanquished, not reconciled. (*b*) The work of salvation is God's (NEB rightly, "God has reconciled you to himself"). By the framework of 1:12-14 and 1:21ff. the hymn is thus kept from becoming a "christomania," a frenzied emphasis on Christ operating apart from the Father's will and plan.

In v. 21 **estranged and hostile in mind, doing evil deeds,** explains as the hymn never had, why "reconciliation" was needed. The enmity was on the side of humankind; the thoughts and deeds of men and women were against God. But God acted through Christ, **in his "body" of "flesh" by his "death";** here we have an exposition of **by the blood of his cross** in v. 20. The phrase "body of flesh" is unusual, though not without parallel (especially at Qumran), and has often been taken as an emphasis on the incarnation (against docetism, the belief that the Son of God merely "appeared" in the flesh); but if anything, its nuance here, besides that of a genuine death on the cross, is of Jesus' physical body as distinguished from **the body, the church** (v. 18). We are also introduced to an early Christian contrast between "before" and "after" the gospel in the words **once** and **now** (cf. Gal. 4:8-9; Rom. 6:17-22; 7:5-6; 11:30; 3:21; Eph. 2:1-10, 11-22). If there is any note of "new creation" in v. 21-22 (cf. v. 23, **creature**), then we may also have reflection of vv. 15*b*, 16*a* and *f* (all involving the terms "create" or "creation") in the hymn.

A note of further purpose not heard in vv. 15-20 is struck by the words in v. 22 that God acted **in order to present you holy and blameless and irreproachable before him.** The first two adjectives are cultic terms, used of sacrificial animals, as on the Day of Atonement (Exod. 29:37-38; Num. 6:14; 1 Peter 1:19); the third one, **irreproachable,** is, however, a legal term ("innocent"; cf. 1 Cor. 1:8), suggesting a court hearing or the day of judgment. The verb **present** fits either imagery (cf. also Rom. 12:1; Jude 24). The whole phrase moves the results of reconciliation into the realm of ethical response on how Christians, now reconciled, are to live. Verse 23 adds a proviso, **provided that you continue in the faith,** i.e., in the gospel they have received, **stable and steadfast, not shifting from the hope of the gospel** (cf. 1:5) **which you heard.** This image of "stability," echoing Qumran and Paul (cf. 1 Cor. 3:10-11, 16-17; 15:58, verses which teach that Christ and gospel are the foundation of the steadfast church community), points ahead to 2:7 where the thought is amplified. It also reflects 1:17*b*, for **all things hold together** through Christ in the new creation as in the old. A final note in v. 23 is the link to the next section about missionary advance of the gospel through the ministry of Paul. That the gospel already **has been preached by every creature under heaven** (cf. 1:20*b*) would be hyperbole. But to read the definite article (as in some mansucripts) and render as "the whole creation" (NEB), as if Paul contemplated preaching to the birds, like Francis of Assisi, and to the rest of nonhuman creation, misses the contrast in vv. 21ff. of "human creatures" to "all things" in 20*a*. Paul's work is viewed here in its universal human scope, from the standpoint of the End. To call him "**minister** of the gospel" both relates Paul to other Christian leaders (1:7; 4:7) and suggests, when coupled with what follows (cf. 1:25, "minister of the church"), his particular apostolic role (1:1).

Continuing to Advance the Word of God to the Gentile World (1:24-29)

Paul now speaks for the first time in the letter in the first person, **I rejoice** ("I" in vv. 24-25, 29, and 2:1-5). In this account of the meaning of his apostolic ministry there is also one verse (28) in the first person plural, **we proclaim,** including his missionary assistants like Timothy (1:1), Epaphras (1:7), and Tychicus (4:7-8). Two other verses (26-27) further describe the gospel; it is **the mystery . . . God chose to make known** now about **Christ** as **the hope of glory.** Reflections of the hymn are fewer and more subtle than in 1:21-23 and 2:8-15, but **his body, that is, the church**

(v. 24) defines "body" exactly as did the addition at 1:18*a*. Cf. also on vv. 26 and 27 below. The majestic language of the passage is clear in its overall intent: Christ advances to his proper preeminence in the world of men and women through the missionary proclamation and labors of Paul and those like him.

With its opening paradox (**rejoice/sufferings**) and a certain parallelism, 1:24 continues the theme of Paul's ministry with one of the most controverted verses in the Bible:

Now I rejoice	**in my sufferings**	**for your sake,**
and in my flesh I complete	**what is lacking in Christ's afflictions**	**for the sake of his body, the church.**

Christ's afflictions are not simply our sufferings *for* Christ (though all Christians may be called upon to suffer for him, 2 Cor. 1:5-7). They are in no sense *like* Jesus' passion, for the Greek word here is never used in the New Testament of his passion. Attractive as it is, with Augustine, to say Christ the head is so identifying with "the members" of his body that "their sufferings are his," the passage seems to deal with Paul (not every Christian) and his sufferings **for . . . the church.** A "passion mysticism" of some sort, whereby there is a "mystical union" binding Christ and the elect together in suffering, has been assumed by other commentators (cf. Phil. 3:10). We come closer to a solution when it is observed that the Greek is literally "the afflictions of *the* Christ," of the Messiah, and hence the allusion is not to the historical Jesus but to a Jewish apocalyptic notion of a quota of "messianic woes" to be endured before the new age comes ("the travail of the Messiah" in rabbinic texts; cf. Mark 13:8, 19-20, 24; Acts 14:22). There is now wide agreement, after centuries of Protestant-Catholic dispute, that nothing was lacking in the atoning sacrifice of Christ on the cross (1:20, 22). Rather, Paul here in apocalyptic terms sees his labors and sufferings as contributing to a "quota" of afflictions assigned before the End can come. **I**

complete, he says, in the sense of "fulfill," a unique service as apostle to the Gentiles, and in that he rejoices at a ministry **in flesh** and deeds (cf. 1:10) as well as words. In favor of this interpretation is the apocalyptic language in vv. 26ff., **hidden/made manifest** and **mystery.**

Paul's role as **minister** (v. 26) is **according to the divine office which was given** him by God for the Colossians (**you**) and for **the Gentiles** (v. 27). Some have sought to take the word rendered as **divine office** in RSV (literally, "the *oikonomia* of God") as a reference to "God's plan of salvation," but that is better expressed by the term **mystery.** Instead, the **office** stresses that Paul is a "steward" (cf. 1 Cor. 4:1; 9:17) entrusted with administration or the carrying out of his functions as suffering apostle-missionary in God's gospel-plan. (Eph. 1:10; 3:2,9 will further develop the sense of this word.) His special function is **to make the word of God fully known** (v. 25) and with others to **proclaim, warning** and **teaching every man** (v. 28, thrice repeated; "every person," universal emphasis again) so as to **present** (cf. 1:22) each one **mature in Christ.**

This last phrase (**mature** = "perfect" in KJV), plus **in all wisdom,** and the word **mystery** have often been taken as gnostic or mystery cults language. But these now can be shown to have Old Testament-Jewish roots. For **wisdom,** see on 1:9 above, and for **mature** see Deut. 18:13 and compare Qumran usage. Not secret Greek cults but Jewish apocalyptic is the background of *mystērion,* as in Dan. 2:28-20 and at Qumran for a secret of God now openly revealed. The pattern **hidden**/revealed (RSV **made manifest**), then/**now,** is paralleled in 1 Cor. 2:7-10; Rom. 16:25-26; and elsewhere. Of course, some of these words may have been terms the false teachers of 2:8ff. paraded about, but the definition of the content of **this mystery** (v. 27) as **Christ in you** (*not* "in each person's heart" but "among you," as proclaimed and present within the community), **the hope of glory** (cf. 1:5,23) is quite Pauline. The word **glory** may distantly reflect "**image**" in the hymn (v. 15), if "the image of its creator" (3:10) and the glory God intended for human beings (Rom. 3:23) is what is being renewed in the "new creation" (2 Cor. 6:4-6; Eph. 4:24). And since **the mystery** is **Christ, hidden for ages and generations** (which the RSV note takes as "hidden from angels"—cf. the "heavenly forces" of 1:16*de*—"and [generations of] men"), we have another implication of Christ's preexistence earlier implied at 1:15. In the phrase **his saints** (v. 26) we are not inclined, however, to see the "heavenly forces" of 1:16 or an inner group of Gnostic charismatics (cf. 1 Cor. 2:6) at Colossae, but the whole congregation there (1:2).

For the spread of this revealed gospel, Paul, given his specially assigned role, says, **I toil** (same verb used for his secular work, 1 Cor. 4:12, cf. Acts 18:3, but here also for his evangelism efforts), **striving with all the energy which he** (God) "energizes" **in me** (cf. 1:11,12 on God "strengthening with all strength" and "empowering" the Colossians). God swept Paul into his unique apostolic role; the apostle in turn seeks to sweep the Colossians on into their appointed ministry as part of the missionary body of Christ. Do they know how much they are on his mind as he labors?

Paul and the Colossians: Personal Resumé (2:1-7)

The first-person style continues, even though **I want you to know** is a Pauline formula (cf. 1 Cor. 11:3) that marks a turn in the letter (as if to say, "Now hear this . . ."), even as Paul sums up **all the riches** (2:2, cf. 1:27) of the gospel of "Christ alone." For along with the prayerlike language of vv. 2-3 (cf. 1:3-8,9-11,12-14) there also breaks surface an ominous allusion to those who **may delude you with beguiling speech.** Against them Paul appeals for **good order and . . . firmness of . . . faith** (2:5). Thus the apostle is **warning** and **teaching** (1:28) as he proclaims Christ. Verses 6-7 offer another summary of the foundations. Because of the introductory formula in v. 1 and the reference to false teachers, some expositors see "the battle against heresy" beginning at 2:1 or 2:4 or 2:6. We regard the section as a transition to the polemic in 2:8ff., but still centered on Paul's particular ministry and reiteration of the gospel on the basis of which he will then speak against the false teachers. It is characteristic of Colossians that much of the material, especially vv. 2-3, 5, is cast as fervent hope (cf. 1:5, 27).

The phrase **how greatly I strive for you** (2:1) picks up on the previous verse **I toil, striving** (1:29; literally "contesting, . . . how great a contest I am engaged in," an athletic metaphor). The apostle's strenuous efforts are not only **for you** at Colossae but also **for those at Laodicea** (cf. 4:13, 15, 16, a neighboring city) and, surprisingly, **for all who have not seen my face** (literally also the Greek adds "in the flesh," as in KJV). If Paul is striving, as he writes, to create a relationship with believers in the Lycus Valley, he also sees his ministry as important for an even greater audience. Paul's "presence" (cf. 2:5) extends beyond where he is physically. We are here on the way to a catholic (worldwide) significance for the apostle to the Gentiles.

From his efforts for them and the gospel, Paul sees the outcome as **their hearts** (the inmost self of all these people, not just those at Colossae) being **encouraged** (cf. 4:8, a constant function in Christian ministry). Encouraged to what? The next verb can mean "instructed in love" (cf. 1 Cor. 2:16 for that sense), as the Vulgate, a few commentators, but no modern translation, render it; it more likely means here "united" or **knit together in love,** because of the use of the term in that sense at 2:19 and 3:14 (love = the bond of perfection). Paul is appealing for a closing of the ranks to face the onslaught of false teaching (cf. Phil. 1:27; 2:2, where the mood is quite similar).

The goal beyond this is expressed by two parallel phrases: so as **to have** (*a*) **all the riches of assured understanding** (the words repeat terms from 1:27, **riches,** and 1:9, **understanding,** but could reflect a concatenation of ideas from the false teachers) and (*b*) **the knowledge** (cf. 1:9) **of God's mystery** (cf. 1:26-27), **of Christ.** The terseness of this last phrase gave rise to many variants in Greek manuscripts, such as that in KJV, "the mystery of God, and of the Father, and of Christ." It has also caused many interpretations, including the attempt to take "**Christ**" in apposition to, that is, as an equivalent of, **God.** In light of 1:27, the sense must be "the mystery of God, that is, Christ." To clarify and enhance Christ as God's revealed mystery, v. 3 weaves in the only Old Testament citation thus far in Colossians, **in whom are "hid" all "the treasures of wisdom" and of knowledge.** Though some deny that the five words in quotation marks above reflect Prov. 2:3-6, we likely have language from Israel's tradition about Wisdom, perhaps applied by the false teachers at Colossae to what they offered. *Solus Christus*, Paul insists, in Christ is all.

When we have Paul's first direct statement about the threat of false teaching, in v. 4, **I say this in order that no one may delude you with beguiling speech, this** refers back to what he just said in pointed resumé. The noun translated **beguiling speech** may be a term the opponents used of their own words, in the sense of "persuasive speech." Paul views them as "talking over" or "deceiving" Christians into errors of doctrine and life-style. His battle against them (as with battles in subsequent years and centuries) Paul must fight through his letters, **absent in body, yet . . . present in spirit** (v. 5; cf. 1 Cor. 5:3; Phil. 1:27).

His hope for the Colossians (**you . . . your**) and all readers is for **good order** (military term) **and** steadfast **faith in Christ.** They **received Christ** (the verb connotes "receive [apostolic] tradition," 1 Cor. 15:1; Gal. 1:9) **just as . . . taught** through Epaphras and others; now **live in him** (literally "walk 'in Christ' and their confession that '**Jesus** is **Lord**' "). The four participles (in the Greek), **rooted, built up, established, abounding,** all describe a growing, well-founded, thanks-giving community, just what is needed for the vicissitudes of Christian life. **Him** (Christ), **the faith,** and **thanksgiving** intertwine in vv. 6-7 as they have in 1:9—2:7. Paul is again **rejoicing** (2:5; 1:24) as he sees (2:5) the Colossian church. But he also sees something menacing.

■ Polemics (2:8-19)

Holding to the gospel of the all-sufficient Christ and his cross,
we oppose deceitful judgments on our liberty and seek to grow
in Christ together.

The polemical heart of the Colossian letter in chap. 2 has been
obscured sometimes by excessive attention to 1:15-20, the hymn
that serves both to help lay Paul's Christological foundation for
the dispute *and* to introduce some of the themes that, treated in
a one-sided way, the opponents embraced. To that extent, 1:15-
20 points precisely to chap. 2. The polemical section (2:8-19) is
flanked by prior reference to the "error" and "specious arguments" (2:4 NEB) of the alien philosophy and even to some of
its catchphrases (2:2-3) and afterwards in the ethical section by
examples of its legalistic preceptions which Paul combats (2:21-
23). Thus, in effect, the deceitful teaching which the epistle op-
poses shapes some of the "foundational" and part of the "paraenetic" (moral admonitions and encouragement) sections.

In some ways the "shape" of Colossians is most reminiscent of
the structure of Philippians as that epistle (possibly combining
three letters) now stands.[11] Instead of just the typical sequence
of "indicative" and "imperative" (or doctrinal assertion followed
by ethical implications), we have in these two letters a foundational assertion of the gospel, including some ethical imperatives
(Phil. 1:1—2:30; note 1:27—2:5 as paraenesis), with a hymn fig-
uring prominently in the argument (Phil. 2:6-11). Then comes a
polemical segment (Phil. 3:2ff., even beginning with the same
verb as at Col. 2:8, **See to it** = "look out!") which merges into
a concluding ethical section (Phil. 3:17; 4:1ff.).

The polemic in Colossians against a teaching that threatens to
undermine the gospel falls into two distinct paragraphs: 2:8-15
treats Christological or doctrinal aspects of the opposing philosophy; 2:16-19 focuses on ascetic practices associated with the new
movement. Paul's protest against its legalistic regulations in ethics
will spill over into the verses following (2:20*b*-23; cf. 14 and 16).

In reading the section we again find phrases of the "Christ hymn" amplified and corrected. Thus **the elemental spirits of the universe** (2:8), whatever it means, no doubt reflects 1:16*de*, "thrones, dominions, principalities, authorities." The difficult statement at 2:9, **"in him" "the whole fulness"** of deity **"dwells" "bodily,"** seems so inescapably intertwined with 1:19 that RSV's translation there, we saw, is colored by 2:9; 1:19 has **"in him"** all the fulness [exactly the same Greek as **the whole fulness**] . . . was pleased to **"dwell,"** and of course **body** occurred at 1:18*a*. At 2:10 **fulness . . . in him** recalls 1:19 again. In the same way 2:10 **the head of all rule and authority** echoes both 1:18, "the head," and 1:16, **"principalities** [literally "rulers"] **or authorities."** When 2:15 refers again to **principalities and powers,** it is more of the same ("powers" is the word in Greek rendered as "authorities" at 1:16*e*). Thus the hymn continues its influence through 2:15, even though Paul will downright contradict it at times.

For following the argument it is also advantageous to mark, perhaps in red, the slogans or key words of the opponents as we try to delineate them. These likely include **philosophy, tradition,** and **elemental spirits of the universe** (2:8); **fulness** (vv. 9 and 10); **all rule and authority** (v. 10) and **principalities and powers** (v. 15); **circumcision** (v. 11); and possibly other phrases like **putting off the body of flesh** or **legal demands** in vv. 11-15, as well as **food and drink, festival, new moon,** and **sabbath** (v. 16) and the several practices listed in v. 18. We shall call attention to this vocabulary of the opponents by use of bold face italics below.

So many preliminary remarks might be thought to exhaust the substance of the sections. As a matter of fact, as more than one commentator has remarked, while the general line of the argument is quite clear, details often elude us. Not least is the question of the identity of the opponents. We do not precisely know, save that they syncretistically combined Jewish elements with pagan-oriental thought possibly native to the Lycus Valley, and factors that might be called "Gnostic."

Christ as Sole and Sufficient Savior (2:8-15)

The gist of the argument of the opponents must have been that
the Pauline gospel as preached by Epaphras does not deliver the
fulness of life possible through their **tradition** or **philosophy** and
certain practices they know, which could put one in touch with
angels and all the forces of heaven. **Circumcision,** a cultic cal-
endar (v. 16), asceticism, and **visions** were all involved in their
program.

Our epistle replies: Christ alone and your Baptism into him
are totally sufficient. The discussion of the meaning of Christ's
cross and our Baptism is presented in creedal language about
Jesus' death and resurrection as reapplied to believers (cf. Rom.
6:3-4): **buried . . ., raised . . .** by **God who raised him from the
dead.** Some think another hymn underlies the section, at least
in vv. 14-15:

Having canceled the bond,
nailing it to the cross,
he made an example of . . . the principalities and powers,
triumphing publicly.

Others include in this hypothetical hymn all of vv. 13-15, from
the words **having forgiven us** to **in him** except for the phrase **with
its legal demands** in v. 14. But there is not the degree of con-
sensus about a hymn here that exists among critics concerning
1:15-20.

In Paul's typical style the opponent or opponents are not
named, but their teachings are described as Paul understands
them (for parallels to **no one** in v. 8 cf. Gal. 1:7 and 2:12, "certain
men" or "some one"). They call their message a *philosophy* and
tradition. Paul adds **empty deceit** and **human** to describe their
tradition (contrast v. 6 on the "apostolic tradition"). He fears that,
like modern sects, the group will **make a prey** of the Colossians;
the verb suggests "kidnap" or "carry off captive in a war" (cf. his
closing martial metaphor in v. 15). They teach **according to** (their)
tradition, **according to** *the elemental spirits of the universe,* **and
not according to Christ.** The middle phrase (cf. Gal. 4:3) is the
difficult one. While it could denote "elements" of which the world

is made or "elementary teachings," it must have referred to the
heavenly powers thought to control so much of ancient life in
conjunction with the heavenly bodies (cf. modern superstitions
about horoscopes).

Apparently the opposing group promised ways one could get
"filled with **fulness**" by their rites and practices, perhaps involving the *plēroma* of heavenly powers (see on 1:19 above). Paul
replies (v. 9) that only in Christ **the "fulness" of deity** (a strong
term, "the divinity"), **"dwells,"** and when he adds **bodily** the
reference is not to the church and certainly not to the world, as
in the hymn, but to the reality and actuality of God in Jesus
Christ. Christ is **the head** of all existing powers in the heavens,
so there is no need to traffic with them for salvation (v. 10; cf.
15, they will not be **"reconciled,"** as in the hymn, but overcome).

The reference in v. 11 twice to **circumcision** sounds Jewish.
But unlike Paul's collision over the practice with the "Judaizers"
in Galatians (cf. esp. 5:2-4), the rite of cutting away the foreskin
of males is not here looked on as a symbol of obedience to Mosaic
law but likely was a kind of sacramental rite leading to more of
the promised "life" (as RSV has added at v. 10 to convey what
"fulness" meant for the group). No need, Paul says, for **you were
circumcised with a circumcision made without hands,** i.e., Christian Baptism (cf. vv. 12-13). The contrast is not with the Jewish
practice but with the group's ritual at Colossae. But the argument
is complicated by a reference to **the circumcision of** (the) **Christ.**
It has frequently been argued, especially by Anglo-Saxon biblical
scholars, that this refers, as the **putting off** of **the body of flesh,**
to Jesus' death on the cross, further described then in 2:15 as a
"discarding of the cosmic powers like a garment" or a "stripping
off of his physical body" (cf. NEB text and note).[12] Then the daring
thought would be that just as Christ put off the alien powers at
his circumcision-death, so you prove victorious over all such powers in your circumcision-death—Baptism. The sense is dramatic,
but for most commentators the results are too abrupt in the sequence of the argument in vv. 11-15. We are content with a
baptismal reference in v. 11, elaborately described first in terms

from the opponents, followed by more conventional liturgical-creedal language. The phrases of 2:15 can be otherwise explained. The emphasis of 2:11 is our **circumcision** (Baptism) **in** and from **Christ, made** by God, not by the **hands** of the Colossian sectarians.

The main verbs and their dependent participles in vv. 10-13, including 11, are regularly second person plural, referring to a single past action, i.e., Baptism:

v. 12   **You were buried with him** [Christ] **in baptism, in which you were also raised with him** . . . [by God].

v. 13   **And you** [direct object] **. . . God made alive together with him.**

To that clear statement are prefaced the references to Baptism using phrases of the opponents:

v. 11   **In him** [Christ] **also you were** *circumcised* [by God];

v. 10   **You have come to** *fulness* **of life in him** [literally, "are 'fulfilled' " in Christ].

This passage goes further than Paul does in Romans, for Col. 2:12-13 speaks of those whose new life was begun at Baptism as being already raised. Paul, at Rom. 6:4-5, refrains from saying that we, like Christ, are raised; he prefers there to emphasize the ethical aspect instead, "that we might walk in newness of life," and then to speak about our resurrection as future. If in Col. 2:10-13 there is a fuller development of Paul's view in Romans, it is probably because the "overly-realized eschatology" of the opponents—their emphasis on the presence now of all future salvation—forced the reply to the Colossians in this direction. They spoke of "having been fulfilled" now by their supplements to Christ; the epistle answers that there is fulfillment and new life solely by Baptism in Christ. It insists this gift is God's work, by **faith in the working of God** (v. 12), and the eschatology has been safeguarded by the stress on hope (1:5, 27).

With v. 13 the construction has not only shifted, as observed above, from "you" to "God" as subject (RSV rightly adds **God,** though KJV is literally correct in saying "he"), but we have moved away from phrases of the opponents (unless *the uncircumcision*

of your flesh is still one) to the language of a Christian community
confessing its sins and receiving forgiveness (**having forgiven us
all our trespasses;** note the shift from **you** in 13*a* to **us** in 13*c*)
and to the possibly hymnic lines of vv. 14-15 (see above). Nonetheless, the figures used are vivid and complex.

The first one in v. 14 about **the bond which stood against us**
most likely refers to a "certificate of indebtedness." This is not
like a pact that Faust (or Adam) made with the devil, but an IOU:
"God, we owe you everything and promise to pay. [Signed] The
daughters and sons of Adam and Eve."[13] **This,** to use a second
figure of speech, God **canceled** (erased, blotted out), **this he set
aside** (he has taken it away, it has no validity and is destroyed).
The third picture in v. 14 is of God **nailing it to the cross.** Here
the "story" of Good Friday is really told as a theological poet
might: humans did not nail Jesus to the cross; the real meaning
is that God was nailing our corporate IOU to the tree and thus
destroyed it.

Not all is neat and tidy, however, when the images flow so hot
and heavily. It has been suggested that **the bond** refers to a personal, penitential confession such as have been found on rock-
cut inscriptions in Asia Minor; therefore, "the autograph of our
self-condemnation in all its detail."[14] If so, Christ wiped it away.
Or the work could mean "the handwriting" (KJV) or "record" of
our evil deeds kept in a book for the judgment. If so, Christ has
set aside this judgment book. Just what **its legal demands** are
depends on how we take the related term **bond.** They could be
the "ordinances" (KJV) or lending law on which the IOU was
based, or more likely "the regulations" (cf. 2:20) which the opponents try to impose; it has even been suggested that they are
indictments of humankind by the angelic powers, demonic ordinances **against us.** To get over the difficulty of how **the bond**
or record book was done away with by **nailing it to the cross,** it
has even been proposed that Christ was the bond thus nailed to
the cross, his body bearing our sins (cf. the gnostic *Gospel of
Truth* 20:23ff.). The general drift of these metaphors as good news
for sinners is clear, even if we cannot sort out exactly all their

imagery, complicated as it is by use of hymn, opponents' ideas, and polemic.

Verse 15, as RSV translates it, presumes a military victory (cf. the language also in vv. 5, **good order,** and 8, **makes a prey of you**) in the phrase **disarmed** the heavenly powers. It then suggests the triumphal procession of a Roman emperor, such as the Arch of Titus records for the victory over Jerusalem in A.D. 70, in the words, God **made a public example of them, triumphing over them in him** (Christ). RSV's footnote rendering implies taking "Christ" as subject of **disarmed** and the other verbs, with the final phrase **in it** referring to the cross. We have already, in connection with 2:9, called attention to the possibility of taking the first verbal form in v. 15 not as **disarmed** but as "discarded the cosmic powers and authorities like a garment" (NEB), like the robe steeped in the blood of the centaur Nessus which Deianira gave to Heracles to hold his love; unlike the Greek myth (where the robe clung to Heracles and poisoned him), Christ stripped it away in triumph. Or (NEB note): Christ "stripped himself of his physical body," so that the "stripping away" of the foreskin in "the circumcision of Christ" is a reference to his death—a view more difficult to accept than either of the first two. Also possible: he stripped the heavenly forces of their authority, like disgraced courtiers.

However we unpack all these figures, God has triumphed utterly in Christ and his cross, and the totality of that victory is available to us in Baptism as new life.

The Result Is Freedom (2:16-19)

Because the alien philosophy threatening Colossian Christianity found Christ inadequate as Savior it offered additional devices to "get through" to the fulness of salvation. Paul warns against anything that bids to supplement **faith in the working of God** through Christ (2:12).

Again the unnamed protagonists' teachings are reflected, this time in five areas: **in questions of food and drink** (probably asceticism and fasting, cf. v. 23, certainly not kosher laws) **or with**

regard to a festival (annual?) **or a new moon** (monthly) **or a sabbath** (weekly). All these calendrical terms are found in the Old Testament (e.g., Ezek. 45:17) and at Qumran, but the Colossian sectarians likely connected their eclectic practices with "the heavenly forces" (2:8, those **elemental spirits of the universe**). On such claims **let no one pass judgment on you,** i.e., make rules. The opening **therefore** in v. 16 shows that these comments by Paul against cultic legalism grow out of the statements on Christology in vv. 8-15. Verse 17 is an appended aside, contrasting such sectarian rules with apostolic Christianity, in terms of **shadow** and **substance,** according to RSV, a contrast going back to Platonic philosophy: **these are only a shadow of what is to come; but the substance belongs to Christ.** Christ's is the "(solid) reality" (NEB, TEV). Since the Greek is literally "but the body (is) of the Christ" (cf. 1:18*a*), some see here a reference to the church (NAB: "the reality is the body of Christ").

In vv. 18-19*a*, a series of characteristic emphases of the false teacher(s) is listed: **let no one disqualify you** (condemn you, decide against you as an umpire might), **insisting on self-abasement and worship of angels, taking his stand on visions, puffed up without reason by his sensuous mind and not holding fast to the Head** (Christ). The final two participial constructions need little explanation, **puffed up, not holding fast.** The errorists are proud of their *fulness* and *knowledge,* but lose Christ as their **"Head"** (1:18*a*). The first participle, **insisting on,** is literally "wishing in" and could mean "taking pleasure in" as a Hebrew idiom (so NIV) or could be taken with the main verb and mean "willfully condemn you." RSV implies that the opponents are bent on forcing three practices on the Colossians. The first, literally "humility" (cf. KJV), has long misled readers because normally the quality is one Paul recommends (e.g., Phil. 2:3; Col. 3:12, "lowliness"); here it is a virtue the opponents cultivate. Translations try to bring out this undesirable nature by "false humility" (TEV) or **self-abasement.** It could, in Jewish pietistic circles, be as specific as "fasting" (Moffatt), or may mean ready compliance to the sect's rules. **Worship of angels,** the second practice, has long been taken to imply veneration of angelic beings, but evidence is scarce for such a practice. The case for the alternative, participation in the (heavenly) worship *by* angels, is attractive; the **devotion** of v. 23 could mean human efforts to participate in such angelic liturgies. The third practice is most baffling, **taking his stand on visions,** literally "going into (detail about) what he has seen" or "entering into (the sanctuary)" in a mystery cult. KJV manuscripts added a negative, "intruding into those things which he hath *not* seen," because the claim of the heretics was not understood. Sober commentators have been reduced to conjectures such as "treading the air" with "empty speculations." A sequence of **self-abasement** (fasting), entering heaven, and sharing the angelic **worship** is an attractive interpretation of the way to ultimate salvation being taught at Colossae beyond mere faith.

To follow such techniques cuts one off from Christ (v. 19). If v. 16 is less than certain as an allusion to the church, v. 19 is not, for it is about **the whole "body"** dependent on **"the Head,"** being **nourished and knit together** (cf. 2:2) **through its joints and ligaments** ("body" analogy!), as it **grows with a growth that is from God.** Eph. 2:21; 4:15-16 repeat and develop this body metaphor together with the picture of the church as a temple.

■ Ethics (2:20—4:6)

Applying the gospel of Christ and freedom with discipline in life, we pursue the way of the Crucified and Risen One in matters great and small.

Pauline epistles regularly lead up to a section on how to realize the new life in Christ in quite practical, everyday ways. Often the apostle employs rather standard paraenetic material such as was delivered to believers at Baptism but which needed reiteration time and again. In various ways this material might be adapted to the specific situation at hand. Always the imperatives grow out of the indicatives of the gospel about what God has done for us.

In Colossians, commentators often see the ethical section as beginning at 3:1, **if then you have been raised with Christ,** followed by the imperative **seek. . . .** In part, this is because of the word **then** at 3:1 (cf. Rom. 12:1, "therefore"). But since the same word occurs at 3:5 and 12 (RSV **therefore, then**) and a few manuscripts and correctors have supplied it at 2:20 (cf. KJV "wherefore"), that "clue" is not decisive. (In Philippians the transitional *therefore* occurs in Greek as early as 2:1, RSV "so.") Commentators on Colossians who place the shift at 3:1 sometimes further remark that reasons for the transition there are not easy to discern. It is better therefore to follow the structural parallelism of the epistle:

2:20   **If with Christ you died** (in Baptism). . ., **why . . . live as if . . .?**

3:1   **If then you have been raised with Christ, seek the things . . . above.**

The first section is negative (2:20-23), against the sectarians' rules; the second (3:1-4) is positive, on Christian life now and to come. The structure grows out of the traditional Pauline language, **buried with Christ/made alive with him** (cf. Rom. 6:4; 4:17; 8:11) as developed at Col. 2:12-13. Grasping the structure of "resurrection life" but not without "death" helps keep us from exaggerating the prominence of 3:1-4 in our letter.

Of course, the polemic against the false teachers of the group in Colossae appears strongly in 2:21-23, but we can presume that countering their inroads was not absent from our writer(s)' mind as the positive section and indeed 3:5ff. were developed. A congregation that withstands the lures of heretical doctrine and practice must not only be solidly grounded but also functioning and growing in a healthy way (cf. 2:19, the missionary body must be sound!). Hence, while using much traditional language from baptismal paraenesis, the letter reveals an awareness of threatening errors. This is seen in the way material is presented (cf. esp. on 3:5, 8) on "the new humanity" (3:5-11), on principles for life in the worlds of family and society (3:18—4:1), and on local ministry and worldwide mission (4:2-6). The part on life together in the church and on worship (3:12-17) looms especially significant for a church threatened by new proposals to deliver nothing less than worship with the angels in the heavens (see on 2:18).

Stereotypical Christian ethics of the first century, often drawn from the best in paganism as well as from Old Testament-Jewish sources, restated in the face of a heresy which we cannot always fully identify; plus the slight but perceptible shift from Paul's futuristic eschatology (as in Rom. 6:5) to one that must stress life now while still trying to hang on to the hope of "what is to come" (1:5,27; 2:17)—all this may make some sentences in Colossians seem less than immediately relevant to us today. But Paul's main point stands: the gospel of new life always has implications for daily life; **therefore** actualize it day by day in your mind's eye vision of God's universe and in how you treat others.

If Dead with Christ in Baptism, You Need No Rules to Aid Salvation (2:20-23)

The condition **if . . .** (v. 20) is assumed to be correct: **you** did die (**died,** single past act) **with Christ** in Baptism. Then you are liberated from those **elemental spirits of the universe** (2:8) in which the false teaching set so much store. So **why . . . live as if you belonged to the world** supposedly dominated by such astral forces? **Why . . . submit to** their **regulations?** (The Greek is quite compressed, and the last verb could recall the "legal demands" in 2:14.)

The letter then lists in v. 21 three examples of these esoteric, sectarian rules: "**Do not handle** (literally "touch, take possession of"; what is prohibited here?—handling taboo food? touching [in the sense of having sexual relations with] a woman, as at 1 Cor. 7:1?)! **Do not taste** (forbidden foods and drink? 2:16)! **Do not touch!**" It is ironic that these legalistic regulations Paul condemns were once used in a revival song to instruct Christians against strong drink, "Touch not, taste not, handle not!" The comment in Colossians is that these rules are **according to human precepts**

and doctrines (cf. 2:8, emphasizing **human**; the wording at 2:22 reflects Isa. 29:13 in the Greek, quoted at Mark 7:7 [parallel Matt. 15:9] against legalistic piety). The further comment is that these things the sectarians seek to avoid as defiling are **things which all perish as they are used.** That is, for Paul they are God's good gifts, destined to be consumed by human use, therefore under no taboos (cf. 1 Cor. 9:25-26,31).

Another listing of the opponents' pet ascetic practices follows in v. 23, condemned by the epistle: **These** (regulations, v. 20; five examples will follow) **have indeed an appearance of *wisdom*** (cf. 1:19; here probably a boast of the heretics) **. . . but they are of no value in checking the indulgence of the flesh** (the Pauline put-down). The examples are the first of three cases where a pentad occurs (cf. on 3:5 and 8), and the five phrases are likely sectarian language to which the epistle sometimes gives a further twist:

(1) **Promoting rigor of devotion**—the single Greek word involved occurs here only in the New Testament and seems to have been coined for the occasion. If from the false teachers, it implied the cult worship they had willingly chosen, perhaps their participation in the liturgies of the heavenly powers (cf. on 2:18; TEV, "forced worship of angels"). If from the apostolic author(s), the term takes on a derogatory meaning, "forced piety" (NEB) or "self-designed religion." RSV's rendering, while straddling the issues, is clearer than KJV's "will worship."

(2) **Self-abasement** or legalistic compliance or fasting (as at 2:18).

(3) **Severity to the body,** ascetic rigors (perhaps involving sex and diet; cf. 1 Tim. 4:3 for such practices among heretics).

(4) **Value** in RSV we have already treated as part of an apostolic condemnation. The Greek literally means "honor," and lexicographers have said that it and the next word, **indulgence,** never have adequately been explained in this verse.

(5) **Indulgence:** RSV's footnote rendering, "serving only to indulge the flesh," suggests that there is a problem of meaning. Among alternatives is the suggestion that the false teachers

claimed "honor" or "value" for their practices and a "satisfying" result (cf. KJV; what RSV renders **indulgence** can mean "satiety, gratification"), i.e., the vaunted "fulness" (see on 2:9-10) proffered by the sectarians. These sectarian code words have been woven into a put-down, **of no value,** just "gratification **of the flesh**" in the pejorative sense of one's "lower nature" (cf. 2:18, where the **sensuous mind** is literally "the mind of the flesh").

Those in Christ have **died** to all this.

If Made Alive with Christ in Baptism, Seek the Life from Above (3:1-4)

Positively put, the second result of Baptism, besides death to the old world and to all exercises for attaining to God (2:20-23), is life with Christ. Three times the phrase resounds: **raised with Christ** (v. 1), **your life . . . hid with Christ** (v. 3), **you also will appear with him in glory** (v. 4). The Christ event, consisting of Jesus' death and resurrection, controls the thinking (2:12-13), this time the latter aspect of being "made alive" by God. For all its Christocentricity, however, the passage (like others, cf. 1:12-13) remains theoultimate (everything, including Christ, is located with reference to **God,** vv. 1 and 3).[15] From the resurrection gospel, **then** (v. 1, logical implication), arise the twin imperatives, **seek the things that are above** (v. 1) and **set your minds on the things that are above** (v. 2).

As in v. 20, the condition introduced by **if** is assumed to have been fulfilled—by Baptism. The imperative of v. 1 follows. To **seek** does not mean frantically to search after, as through the devices of the sectarian group, but "set your hearts on" (TEV), "orient your life by" **the things. . .above.** Especially when contrasted with **things that are on earth** (v. 2), that sounds ethereal to modern ears. The language is compelled partly by the sectarian claims about their heavenly contacts, but partly also by the fact that what often in the New Testament is presented as a temporal contrast (before/after, the old and the new age) is here presented spatially. Having died to "the elemental spirits of *the world*," no longer, as it were, "living *in the world*" (2:20, using spatial terms), where else can one associate with the Lord but **where Christ is?** As all Christians know, Jesus, exalted since Easter, is **seated at the right hand of God,** to use an early creedal phrase (ultimately from Ps. 110:1; Acts 2:34; Heb. 1:3). And in the cosmology of the day, that meant in "heaven," **above** the earth. The admonition is not escapist but to "think Christ," crucified and raised, rather than the fleshly, sensual ideas of the false teachers. Cf. also Gal. 4:26, Jerusalem "above," and Phil. 3:14, the call to life "above."

Baptism (**you have died,** v. 3: cf. 2:12) incorporates one into the risen Christ. Col. 3:1 goes further than Paul ever did in Romans 6 in allowing *resurrection* life here and now. Besides the polemical context and ethical direction in which our passage takes the assertion, two qualifications stand out: (1) This **life is hid,** not open (cf. 2:3), and (2) the hope so prominent in Paul, about **when Christ who is our life appears,** continues as a parousia promise for believers: **you also will appear. . .in glory** only at that time, not now. Till then, more admonitions (3:5—4:6).

Imperatives for the New Humanity (3:5-11)

Five imperatives or verb forms that are, in effect, commands provide the structure for this section: **put to death. . .**(v. 5); **put. . .away** (v. 8); **do not lie** (v. 9a); and two Greek participles probably used as imperatives, **put off** (9b) and **put on** (10). All the material is at home in Pauline paraenetic sections. It is obviously baptismal (see on vv. 9-11). But there are signs that it is arranged pertinently to the situation in Colossae. **Put to death** relates to **you died** (2:20; cf. 3:3), and the pair of references keep us from overindulging on **you have been raised** (3:1), the opening in the section they flank. The imperative **put off** (3:9b) is the same verb we met at 2:15 (see note above on **disarmed** as "strip off"); cf. 2:11 **putting off.** In v. 10, **knowledge** is a word we have met before (1:9; cf. 1:6). Does v. 10, **image** and **creator,** relate at all to 1:15a and the "creation" strophe of the hymn, or do the words **Christ is all, and in all** echo the hymn (1:16af, 18d)? The order is thus partly dictated by use of traditional material and partly by relevance to Colossae. The next paragraph, 3:12ff., will move on directly, indeed continuing the theme of 3:10, **put on. . . .**

In v. 5 **therefore** shows that the command to **put to death what is earthly in you** is rooted in the gospel indicative. Baptism puts believers in the realm of Jesus' cross and resurrection; they must appropriate the effects in their lives. RSV comes close to expressing the fact that **what is earthly** is the same phrase as **things. . .on earth** in 3:3 (see explanation there), but RSV omits "your members" (KJV), those earthly-oriented parts of a person's life, five examples of which are named: **immorality** (in sex life; sometimes marriage within forbidden limits of kinship), **impurity, passion, evil desire, covetousness** (the first four have especially to do with sex; the fifth is more general, leading away from God, and hence amounts to **idolatry; covetousness** as a form of **idolatry** is the desire to grasp and control God's gifts as our own possessions). As at Gal. 5:21 and elsewhere, there follows a warning statement (v. 6), **the wrath of God is coming** (cf. 1 Thess. 1:10; Rom. 1:18) **on account of these** activities. That **in these** ways the Colossians **once walked, when** they **lived in them** is further evidence the congregation there was of Gentile background (cf. 1:21; 2:11); these were not Jewish sins (cf. Rom. 1:18-32).

From the use of **once** (v. 7) and **now** (v. 8) one would expect (cf. on 1:21-22) some statement like, "now you no longer walk in these things." But true to the Pauline view of Christians as people who in this life are not yet beyond Sin's attacks and in view of the situation in Colossae, the letter specifically admonishes **now put them. . .away**, and a fresh list of five vices follows: **anger, wrath, malice, slander, and foul talk from your mouth** (the last mentioned may mean obscene stories and ribald remarks, popular even at Greek religious cult festivals). The mouth as well as other members need to "clean up their act." **Do not lie to one another** (9a) follows naturally; mind and mouth must unite in a concern for truth.

It is possible and attractive to take the next two verb forms, as KJV and RSV do, to show the reason why Christians are to act thus: **seeing that you have put off the old nature with its**

practices and have put on the new. There is agreement that **put off** and **put on** reflect the practice in Baptism of taking off one's garments to descend into the water and afterwards of being clothed in a fresh (white) robe. So the sense would be: do these things because you have been baptized! But grammatically each can also be an imperative, as the *Twentieth Century New Testament* took them as long ago as 1904.

In any case one has (and, we suggest is to) put off **the old nature** and **put on the new nature.** The literal KJV rendering "old man/ new man" will not do in a day of sensitivity to problems of sexist language. But **nature** or "self" (TEV) are not satisfactory either, for the Greek terms are corporate and the "new" divinely given, not "natural," so we suggest "humanity." What Adam and Eve were intended to be is the goal. But even for Christians in Colossians, such a goal is not yet achieved (though the false teachers might have thought they had "arrived"). For the new humanity is still **being renewed** (by God), **in knowledge** (of God, 1:10, of Christ and salvation, 2:2; of God's will for their lives, 1:9), **after the image** (cf. Gen. 1:26-27) **of its creator** (God, in Genesis; but in Col. 1:15-20, Christ, who in Pauline thought generally is the only one to possess the image of God; for others, the image is something restored at Baptism, where one becomes not only "saved" but also "human").[16]

Both the baptismal milieu and the emphasis on "the new" in Christ of vv. 9-10 is underscored by a formula of equality and unity in Christ employed at early Christian Baptisms (cf. Gal. 3:27-28; 1 Cor. 12:3). **Here there cannot be Greek and Jew** (the archetypical distinction for Jews), **circumcised and uncircumcised** (the differentiation which the false teachers were trying to bring in at Colossae), **barbarian, Scythian** (a particularly uncouth kind of non-Greek), **slave, free. . .** (economic distinctions). (Presumably "male and female," Gal. 3:28, is unmentioned because such differences were no issue at Colossae.) In his community, **Christ is all** and the call is to a way of life consistent with such a Lord.

Life Together in the Lord Christ's Realm (3:12-17)

A new beginning in the series of imperatives is suggested by **then** (v. 12, cf. 3:1,5) and the address, **as God's chosen ones, holy and beloved** (all three adjectives are Old Testament terms used of Israel, reapplied in the New Testament to Christians). The verb **put on** is, however, the same as at 3:10; it somewhat corresponds to 3:5, "kill" the five kinds of earthly-mindedness listed, for it too is followed by a set of five things, all virtues. We can now also complete the pattern previously noted:

2:12*a*; 2:20   with Christ you died   →   3:5 **Put to death therefore** five things.

2:12*b*-13; 3:1   you have been raised with Christ   →   3:12 **Put on then** the five virtues, all of which are words with a twofold Pauline sense:

used elsewhere of God or Christ (indicative)	*used here of Christians (imperatives)*
(1) **compassion** (Rom. 12:1; 2 Cor. 1:3)	cf. Phil. 2:1, same double phrase, KJV "bowels and mercies";
(2) **kindness** (Rom. 2:4; 11:2)	cf. 2 Cor. 6:6; Gal. 5:22;
(3) **lowliness** (cf. Phil. 2:8 "humbled" with Phil. 2:3)	same Greek word, different sense, at Col. 2:18,23;
(4) **meekness** (2 Cor. 10:1)	Gal. 6:1; like "lowliness" *never* a virtue to Greeks;
(5) **patience** (Rom. 2:4; 9:22)	cf. 1:11; Gal. 5:22.

The rest of this anthology of practical advice for Christians in community hangs on an outline like this:

v. 13   • **forbear(ing) one another,** paralleled by another participle imperative,

        • **forgiving one another,** in case of grudges or grievances.

Indicative-imperative support: **as the Lord** (Christ) **has forgiven you, so you also must forgive.** Then, perhaps just as **do not lie** in v. 9 capped the list of five vices in 3:8, **love** (v. 14) climaxes the five virtues of 3:12. **And above all these** (almost, like a sweater, "on top of them") **put on love** (RSV supplies the verb from v. 12). Love **binds everything together in perfect harmony,** literally, "is the bond [cf. 2:2, 18] of [leading to] perfection [see on 1:29, same root as 'mature']."

v. 15   ● **And let the peace of** (the) **Christ rule in your hearts**
         . . . .

v. 16   ● **Let the word of Christ dwell in you richly . . .,**
         as you teach and admonish (cf. 1:28) **. . .and**
         . . .sing. . . .

Overall imperative: **whatever you do . . ., do everything in the name of the Lord Jesus** (17a).

All Christian life is under this Christological rubric, not forgetting (again) doxology to God, **giving thanks to God the Father through him** (cf. 1:3, 12 and 3:15, **be thankful**).

Woven into these Christ-centered imperatives are evidences of interest in the church (**you were called in the one body to the peace of Christ,** v. 15) and in worship (v. 16, under the word the congregation teaches and admonishes mutually: the triad **psalms and hymns and spiritual songs** we can scarcely distinguish clearly, but a lively worship life in hymns is suggested; cf. 1:15-20 and 2:13-15). One could appropriately go right on to 4:2ff.

Principles and Modifications for Relationships among People in Home and Society (3:18—4:1)

These verses present a neatly structured section on relations between family or economic groups within the social and cultural conditions of the day. Each group is named; an imperative verb addresses a command to it; some motivation or reason usually follows for what is enjoined. The dominant verb, even more so in similar passages at Eph. 5:21—6:9; 1 Tim. 2:8-15 and 6:1-2;

Titus 2:1-10; and 1 Peter 2:13—3:7, is "be subject." In each pairing of two groups, the subordinate group always is mentioned first:

Wives, be subject to your husbands, as is fitting in the Lord (18).
  Husbands, love your wives, and do not be harsh with them (19).

Children, obey your parents in everything, for this pleases the Lord (20).
  Fathers, do not provoke your children, lest they become discouraged (21).

Slaves, obey in everything. . .your earthly masters. . ., knowing that from the Lord you will receive the inheritance as your reward (22-25).
  Masters, treat your slaves justly and fairly, knowing that you also have a Master [Lord] in heaven (4:1).

Commentaries on the other epistles with such sections, especially Eph. 5:21ff., should be compared. Our chief problem today is not the meaning of such passages in detail but their relevance for us, for the temptation is either to dismiss them as impossible for liberated people or to make them into immutable laws for sound marriages, happy homes, and (all too often) the ideal society.

The name *Haustafeln*, "table of rules for households," has been applied to such passages, and the tables were widely disseminated through Luther's Small Catechism. (Luther's explanations often exhibit sensitive applications updated for his day.) "Household duties" will not quite do, however, as a term, because the slave/master situation, not to mention citizen/state relationship (1 Peter 2:13-17), reached into broader society. Hence we suggested in our title "principles" for relations among groups in church and society.

To be noted next, from the very location of these "principles" in Colossians and the other epistles, is the fact that Christians are addressed. But the believers involved might be married to a non-Christian spouse (cf. 1 Cor. 7:12-16) or be slaves of a pagan master (cf. 1 Peter 2:18; 1 Tim. 6:2), so the points set forth must fit in a mixed society and reflect the culture of the day. They do, for these "**be subject** sections" can at many points be paralleled with wisdom teaching found in Greek philosophers, especially the Stoics, Hellenistic Judaism, and even beyond. The best insight of much of the world of the day is thus adopted in these passages.

But the rules or duties are regularly in the New Testament altered in one way or another. This stems (1) from the indicative/imperative context, so that if what is said rests on the gospel of what God has done, then the gospel may modify what is set forth. So here, v. 18, **as is fitting,** suggests social standards of the day, but **in the Lord** (cf. also vv. 20, 22, 23, 24) takes on a different cast when **the Lord Christ** is in the picture. Alteration comes also (2) from the Christian eschatological expectation of a judgment to come. Thus, slaves and masters both have a Lord in heaven who can **reward** or **pay back for the wrong. . .done** (3:24-25; 4:1). Hence one can claim there is modification of the basic scheme by the gospel.

Our example in Colossians is probably the earliest in any New Testament letter. That in Ephesians is more elaborate at many points. But the material is more widespread than the Pauline corpus, and probably was traditional among certain Christians when Colossians incorporated it. If Colossians, Ephesians, and the Pastorals are, as we believe, all deutero-Pauline, then Paul himself never uses the structure concerning husbands and wives, parents and children, etc. All in all, we have a deutero-Pauline use, then, of gospel-adapted social wisdom of the Mediterranean, quite necessary for living the new faith in day-to-day relationships. Here we begin to see how life in such areas was being affected by the gospel. If it did not change things so rapidly as some might hope, it scarcely left things as they were.

The example of slaves and masters receives special attention in Colossians (more lines than the other four groups together). That is because of the reference to come in 4:9 to Onesimus, Philemon's slave (see below). What Colossians says both fits how Paul had handled that case *and* orients Christian slaves to a realistic attitude as faithful servants of masters with a different, non-Christian outlook (cf. v. 22, **not with eyeservice, as men-pleasers** seems coined for this passage and means "don't do just what can be seen superficially, to catch the boss's eye, while cutting corners and not cleaning under the bed or tightening the bolt under the hood").

It is the wife-husband relationship that most attracts interest today. Paul's baptismal equality formula at 3:11 points to the transcending of traditional barriers, and in its form in Gal. 3:28 specifically denies that such distinctions hold "in Christ." For a pluralistic society where subjection of the wife was usual or, in the case of too much flaunting of freedom by women, seemed (to men) to be called for, 3:18-19 reflected a widespread norm. But **in the Lord,** and the use of a command to the husband, above all, to **love,** contained seeds that would blow apart any rigidity to the *Haustafeln* structure. Just as 3:16 enjoined "admonishing **one another**," so Christian spouse and mate would eventually sense the need for mutuality in the home. That view came to specific expression as early as Ephesians, which prefaces its table of relationships with the earthshaking premise, "Be subject *to one another* out of reverence for Christ" (5:21).

Admonitions for Christians in a Missionary Church (4:2-6)

After the *Haustafel* section (3:18—4:1), the general admonitions of 3:12-17 continue. This closing, seemingly miscellaneous collection (cf. 1 Thess. 5:16-22) has a structure that is reflected in RSV's paragraphing, built around two verbs which are common Pauline imperatives, **continue** and **conduct yourselves** (both begin in Greek also with the same letter; cf. Rom. 12:12, "*be constant* in prayer," and 13:13, "let us *conduct* ourselves," same verbs):

v. 2*a*   **Continue steadfastly in prayer,**

v. 2*b*   **being watchful in it with thanksgiving;**

v. 3   **pray**(ing) **for us also. . .,**

v. 4   **that I may make it** [the word] **clear, as I ought to
              speak.**

v. 5*a*   **Conduct yourselves wisely . . .**

v. 5*b*   **making the most of the time. . . .**

v. 6*a*   **speech** [being] **seasoned with salt,**

v. 6*b*   **so that you may know how you ought to answer every
               one.**

The parallelism between the two admonitions is more impressive
when we note that each is thus followed by two participles (all
of them imperatives in force, so that RSV is justified in treating
those in vv. 3 and 6*a* as such). Each paragraph concludes with a
statement about **the word** (v. 3; v. 4 = **it;** v. 6, **your speech**),
the first in vv. 3-4 having to do with Paul, the second in v. 6 with
the Colossians and other readers.

The theme of **prayer** (2*a*) has been frequent (1:3-14), especially
with thanksgiving (4:2; cf. 1:2, 12; 2:7; 3:15, 17). To **continue
steadfastly** suggests persistence (Luke 18:1-8), at any and all
times, not just fixed hours, **watchful** when drowsiness threatens
(cf. Mark 14:37-41) or watchful for the parousia (cf. 1:5; 3:4). The
Colossians are to **pray** specifically **for us also** (not just for themselves, but Paul *and colleagues*), and for the mission of the word:
**that God may open to us a door for the word, to declare the
mystery of Christ** (3*bc*). The second phrase (3*c*) about "declaring
the mystery" explains the word or gospel in terms that the letter
has already used (cf. 1:26-28; 2:2). The prior phrase (3*b*) could in
context imply simply that a door out of jail be opened for Paul
who is **in prison on account** of Christ's **word,** but Pauline usage
(1 Cor. 16:9; 2 Cor. 2:12) clearly means a door of missionary
opportunity. Note that it is an opening for **us** to preach the word,
even though v. 4 is couched in the first person singular, **as I
ought to speak** (the phrase suggests Paul's role in God's plan for

mission, cf. 1 Cor. 9:16; Col. 1:25,29). The pronouns are important for establishing the sequence of "Paul, Paul's missionary helpers, and the Colossian readers" (including us).

This missionary advance of God's plan is also reflected in the second imperative section, vv. 5-6. The readers are to "walk in wisdom" (cf. 1:9-10,28) not just with regard to one another (cf. 3:16) but with regard **toward outsiders** (non-Christians; cf. 1 Thess. 4:12). They do this by (*a*) **making the most of the time** (a difficult phrase, used differently at Eph. 5:16, but here meaning both seizing opportunities and a wise stewardship of every day that God gives), and (*b*) by the very way they speak to other people. Is one's **speech** shaped ultimately by **the word** of God? Is it **gracious** (because of experiences with grace; cf. KJV)? Is it **seasoned with salt** (i.e., to the point, using the right words, not insipid, but wholesome, as commentators have variously suggested; cf. Eph. 4:15)? Does it rightly speak to people (**answer every one**) where they are?

This closing little paraenetic section binds the Colossians to Paul not only in his suffering (1:24) but in his gospel, mission, and life-style.

■ Greetings, News, Links, and Closing Blessing (4:7-18)

Paul's letters regularly conclude with greetings from Paul and those with him, news of his plans, usually a postscript in his own hand (Gal. 5:11ff.), and a benediction (e.g., 1 Thess. 5:26-28; 1 Cor. 16:5-24; Phil. 4:21-23). Colossians is no exception. It is most like Philemon in terms of the persons mentioned by name. It is around these names, from **Tychicus** (v. 7) to **Demas** (v. 14), that the structure, such as it is, of vv. 7-14 can best be viewed. Col. 4:15-17 introduces a reference to a cryptic **letter from Laodicea** among Paul's specific admonitions. The final verse (18) is a succinct 14-word summary in Paul's own hand. The section as a whole is remarkable, however, for its lack of reference to Paul's personal plans or even news of how things are going, compared with, say, 1 Cor. 16:5-9, 2:19-24, or even Philemon 22. The "apostolic presence" in Colossians is not a matter of his expected arrival soon "in person" but of his "spirit" while absent (2:5) and of links through his colleagues in the ministry (4:7-14).

On any reading, these closing paragraphs pose certain problems in conceptualizing the setting for the letter. Where in the Roman empire are all the persons mentioned to be thought of as being present with Paul? Probably the traditional answer—Rome—fits best, but we lack other evidence about the whereabouts of most of them at this time apart from traditions (e.g., Mark). The same applies to Caesarea and Ephesus as places of Paul's imprisonment, the references to **Mark** and **Luke** being especially difficult for Ephesus (see below). Again and again the parallel references in Philemon are our chief clues, seemingly expanded in Colossians. We shall always cite below the Philemon reference after each name in Colossians, and assume that the *dramatis personae* in that little note are the traditional ones (compare below on vv. 9 and 17):

> Philemon, of Colossae, and his wife Apphia
> owned a slave, Onesimus, and had a son, Archippus.[17]

For those who read Colossians as a deutero-Pauline letter, as we do, the references in 4:7-18 raise a problem not always faced: are this parade of eight names, the reference to a Laodicean letter, and Paul's postscripts intended simply to add a degree of verisimilitude to a pseudonymous treatise? One could say that our author(s) has/have put together a montage of Pauline persons and phrases, especially from the names in Philemon (seven or eight names, plus Apphia). Perhaps some verses even derive from genuine fragments of Paul. That might have helped gain a hearing for Colossians, especially with people who knew of the note to Philemon (though scarcely in Colossae itself, unless memories were very short). Hence it has been claimed that there is a further aim: these names, vouchsafed by "Paul's own" comments, are certified as genuinely Pauline (cf. especially vv. 7-8, 9, and 13); thus a "succession" of teachers true to the apostle is provided. This is possible. We are more impressed by the fact that many of the references provide for links to Colossae whereby **Tychicus** and **Onesimus** will come (vv. 7-9), **Mark** may turn up there (v. 10), **Epaphras (one of yourselves,** who seems originally to have evangelized the area) is especially commended, and **Archippus** (v. 17) is possibly designated his successor there. If Paul himself cannot come, these are the ones who will present and preserve his gospel there. The verses therefore serve the purpose of backing up the arguments in the letter itself with a series of persons who in Colossae (and elsewhere) will present in person (and through their writings) the same truths for which Paul stands, when he cannot come because of imprisonment—or death. To this extent there is a "succession," not in "office" (for none of them is "apostle" as Paul was, 1:1, and they are but—yet just as much as Paul—"fellow servants" and "ministers" of the word; cf. 1:7, 23, 25; 4:7, 10, 11, noting use of "fellow" in English), but a succession in the gospel or word or mystery of Christ. In showing how this letter might be followed up at Colossae, the epistle suggests to all readers how Paul's gospel will go on: by his writings and by those who minister as he did for the same gospel.

Tychicus and Onesimus: News from Paul (4:7-9)

The theme of the section is really **all about my affairs** (vv. 7, 9, more literally "all the news about me," TEV, and "all things here"; v. 8, **how we are,** literally, "the things concerning us"). The letter to the Colossians gives no clue as to how good or bad things are with Paul or how he thinks they will turn out; his highly commended messengers (**beloved, faithful,** etc.) will report all that.

Tychicus (not in Philemon), according to Acts 20:4, accompanied Paul as a representative of churches in the province of Asia on the trip to Jerusalem with the collection. Otherwise only Eph. 6:21, in the same words as here, and 2 Tim. 4:12 and Titus

3:12 (both brief references to assignments for Paul) mention him. **Onesimus** is the runaway slave of Philemon who is being sent back to his master by Paul (Philemon 10-21) or at least to his former master's city. It is speculation to suppose that Paul himself wrote Col. 4:9 in order to pressure Philemon through the church there to receive him back without punishment or to free Onesimus; speculation, likewise, to argue this is the Onesimus who, according to Ignatius (*Ephesians* 1:3; 2:1; 6:2), later became bishop of Ephesus. On the other hand, we need not suppose, as Calvin did, that this Onesimus is a different person than the slave in the letter to Philemon. The statement of 4:9 is that Onesimus has been accepted as a helper by Paul.

Greetings from Paul's Missionary Colleagues (4:10-14)

The theme is "so-and-so greets you." Five, maybe all six, individuals are paralleled in the note to Philemon.

● **Aristarchus** (Philemon 24) was, like Tychicus, a companion on Paul's collection visit to Jerusalem (Acts 20:4). A Thessalonian, he is not mentioned in Paul's letters to that city, but only in Acts at Ephesus (19:29) and at Caesarea, where he accompanies Paul on a ship to Rome (27:2). The epithet **fellow prisoner** (of Christ) could be metaphorical (cf. Rom. 16:7).

● **Mark** (Philemon 24) is otherwise mentioned in the Pauline corpus only at 2 Tim. 4:11. Acts refers to him as John Mark and to his mother's house in Jerusalem (12:12, 25), reports his work with Paul on a mission journey to Cyprus, and does not gloss over his defection at Perga (13:13) and Paul's subsequent refusal to take him along on another trip (16:37-40). That Mark was **the cousin of Barnabas** we learn only from this verse, but it would explain why Barnabas split with Paul and sailed away to Cyprus with his relative, Mark (16:39). One other reference has Peter referring to Mark spiritually as "my son" (1 Peter 5:13). He is traditionally credited with writing the second gospel in the New Testament canon. The **instructions** here—**if he comes to you, receive him**—assume a reconciliation with Paul; he is now OK.

• **Jesus who is called Justus** is unmentioned in Philemon unless we construe vv. 23-24 to mean, "Epaphras, my fellow prisoner in Christ, sends greetings to you, (and so do) Jesus, Mark, Aristarchus, Demas, and Luke. . . . " We have no other reference to a man with the then-not-uncommon Jewish name **Jesus** and the Greek name **Justus.** The epithet **men of the circumcision** implies that all three mentioned in vv. 10-11 are Jewish Christians (Aristarchus too!). That **only** these three of the Jews confess Christ and are **fellow workers** sounds a note of pain (cf. Rom. 9:1-3), though the work of these three **for the kingdom of God** makes them all the more **a comfort.**

• **Epaphras** (Philemon 23), previously identified (1:7-8) as the likely evangelizer of the Lycus Valley, including **you** in Colossae and **those in Laodicea and in Hierapolis** nearby, is thought to be the one who brought Paul word both of how well things had gone there (2:5) and of the threatening false philosophy (2:8ff.). Now he is commended (even if he had personally not been up to handling that threat to the faith) because he **worked hard** as a missionary and prayed hard (v. 12) for the Colossians. The gist of his prayers is **that you may stand mature** (cf. 1:22*b*-23; 2:7; 1:28; 3:14) **and fully assured in all the will of God.** The participle **fully assured** may mean only "ripe in conviction" (NEB) but more likely echoes the false teachers' blandishments of "fulness" (2:9-10) as seen by our author(s) to be rightly offered in Christ alone (1:9—here, as there, coupled with God's saving and moral **will**). Not an inappropriate prayer for any leader or member for his fellow believers!

• **Luke** (Philemon 24; cf. 2 Tim. 4:11). The addition here of the description of him as **the beloved physician** makes it the only place in the New Testament that we are told of Luke's M.D. degree. Traditionally he is credited with writing the third gospel and Acts; does Colossians mean to invoke the considerable weight of those two volumes to support the Pauline gospel? The chronology, on most theories of datings, makes that quite uncertain, for it is doubtful that Luke-Acts was written when Colossians was composed. Recent speculation that Luke wrote the Pastoral Epistles as "volume 3" in his works[18] would tie him more closely to the (late) Pauline world.

● **Demas** (Philemon 24) is otherwise known only for the melancholy reference in 2 Tim. 4:10 that he deserted Paul.

Paul's Greetings and Instructions (4:15-17)

Give my greetings uses the same word as in vv. 10, 12, and 14; it could just as well be "give *our* greetings" (NEB, italics added), though most translations and commentators assume that Paul is here adding his own to the list. But literally it is, "salute" (KJV), i.e., you greet **the brethren** (all Christians) **at Laodicea. . . .** That assumes (or asks for) communications between the two communities eight and one-half miles apart. The second greeting (Paul's, the Colossians, or both) is **to Nympha and the church in her house.** The proper name can be feminine or masculine, and textual evidence shows shifts from **her** to "his" (KJV, NEB note) or "their"; most likely, as we are now more willing to recognize, the woman Nympha provided space for (presided over?) a house church (cf. Acts 16:15,40). But where? In Hierapolis (4:13)?

This letter that we call Colossians is to be read first at Colossae (aloud, surely; when the community is gathered together, likely in a worship context) and then **also in the church of the Laodiceans.** Conversely **see that you read also the letter from Laodicea.** The "letter from Laodicea" means one from Paul to that community, a letter which at the time of composition of Colossians is at Laodicea, not one from the Laodiceans to Paul or to Colossae. But what became of it? People over the years have sought it in our canonical Ephesians (cf. the absence of "in Ephesus" in some manuscripts at Eph. 1:1), in Philemon, or even in Hebrews. By the fourth century a letter "To the Laodiceans" existed (extant today only in Latin, in the New Testament apocrypha), harmlessly but stupidly fabricated from genuine Pauline letters.[19] The fact is that "Laodiceans," like some other letters of

165

Paul (cf. 1 Cor. 5:9), has disappeared. We may add: if it ever existed, for the cross-reference *could* be another link to relate the readers of Colossians with the Pauline ambit. Romantic theorists will speculate; we simply have no such document.

Quite specifically, Paul says to **Archippus** in the second person singular, **. . . fulfil the ministry which you have in the Lord.** We may reject the speculation that Archippus was the owner of Onesimus and that "the ministry" Paul asks is for him to send back the slave to Paul as his own! Some translations ecclesiasticize "the ministry" here too much, the nature of which we do not know (e.g., Phillips, "God ordained you to your work—see that you don't fail him"; NEB, ". . . in the Lord's service . . . , discharge it to the full"). If we must guess at the task he has as a Christian, it could be, within the missionary setting of Colossians, somewhere between the general sort of "service" described in 1 Cor. 12:5 and 16:15 and specific later church offices. The "work of an evangelist," as successor to Epaphras in Colossae, perhaps comes closest to it of all New Testament references to service or ministry (cf. 2 Tim. 4:5 where "fulfil your ministry" also occurs).

Personal Postscript (4:18)

As in other letters, Paul adds a closing, taking the pen himself from the professional or more skilled Christian scribe. According to 2 Thess. 3:17-18 (cf. 2:2), the practice helped identify the letter as Paul's own, not a forgery. No attempt is made here, as in Gal. 6:11-18, to reiterate the message of the epistle. Instead we have first his own addition to the list of six names: **I, Paul, write this greeting with my own hand.** Then there is a reminder of his status as prisoner: **Remember my fetters.** Finally, a benediction, liturgical but more terse than in most Pauline epistles: **Grace be with you.** 1 Tim. 6:21 and 2 Tim. 4:22 are exactly the same; Titus 3:15 and Heb. 13:25 add ". . . you *all*." In the circle of Christians at Colossae, at Laodicea, in Nympha's house, in Hierapolis, and each place ever since where Colossians is studied, Paul's concern for fellow believers and his emphasis on the grace of God as the foundation of all Christianity are thus conveyed.

NOTES

1. Cited by Martin H. Scharlemann, "The Great Christology (Colossians 1:15-20)," unpublished paper for the Conference of Lutheran Seminary Professors, June 2, 1964. The reference is to Deissmann's *Paul: A Study in Social and Religious History*, trans. William E. Wilson (2nd rev. ed.; London: Hodder & Stoughton, 1927; reprinted, New York: Harper Torchbooks, 1957; Gloucester, Mass.: Peter Smith, 1972) 107, n. 3. The context is a reference to the sense of "contemplation" in Colossians and Ephesians, seen in Paul's "foaming rhythms" and "dynamically pre-existent cantatas." Deissmann liked to compare Paul and Bach; see his lectures, *The Religion of Jesus and the Faith of Paul* (New York: George H. Doran Company, 1923) 202 and 242.

2. E. Lohse, *Colossians and Philemon* (Hermeneia Commentary; Philadelphia: Fortress, 1971) 84-91, has an excellent section on "The Language and Style of Colossians," listing, for example, the 34 Greek words in Colossians that are found nowhere else in the New Testament, the 28 words found elsewhere in the New Testament but not in any letter by Paul, the 10 words found only in Ephesians and Colossians in the New Testament, and similar details. Eduard Schweizer, *The Letter to the Colossians* (Minneapolis: Augsburg, 1982) 15-19, discusses factors in style and content that give one pause about Pauline authorship, e.g., an "almost complete lack of references to the Spirit." To this observation we may add the absence of Paul's characteristic ideas on righteousness/justification, Sin, law, promise, and even believing; cf. J. Reumann, *"Righteousness" in the New Testament: "Justification" in the United States Lutheran-Roman Catholic Dialogue* (Philadelphia: Fortress, New York: Paulist, 1982) 91-92. For an example of a word in Colossians that takes on a new and significant sense there, compared with meanings it had in earlier, acknowledged letters of Paul, the term rendered in the RSV at 1:25

as "divine office" may be cited; this application seems "the significant and pivotal step" in development of the term's usage, "even more theologically 'advanced' than the Ephesians references" to it (J. Reumann, *"Oikonomia*-Terms in Paul in Comparison with Lucan *Heilsgeschichte," New Testament Studies* 13 [1966-67] 147-67, esp. 161-63).

3. For some significant treatments of the problem over the last century and more, concerning the nature of the "Colossian heresy," see *Conflict at Colossae: A Problem in the Interpretation of Early Christianity Illustrated by Selected Modern Studies,* ed. and trans. Fred O. Francis and Wayne A. Meeks, rev. ed. (SBS 4; Missoula, Mont.: Scholars Press, 1975). More than 100 years ago Bishop J. B. Lightfoot sensed Jewish and Gnostic elements in the Colossian opponents of Paul, akin to Essenism (a position brilliantly confirmed by subsequent examination of the Dead Sea scrolls material, from a group at Qumran certainly related to the ancient Essenes). Later, Martin Dibelius compared the initiation rites in the cult of the goddess Isis. Günther Bornkamm delineated the heresy as arising out of "gnosticized Judaism" with elements of Persian and Chaldean thought, a syncretism represented centuries later in the ideas of the poet Goethe. The Jesuit Stanislas Lyonnet underlined the Jewish and Qumran elements in the "Gnostic" vocabulary of Colossians. The late Fred O. Francis contributed insights from legal papyri, oracles, and other ancient texts for clarifying the "ascetic mysticism" that characterized the opponents' thought. J. Burgess, in *Colossians* (Proclamation Commentaries; Philadelphia: Fortress, 1978) 45, is typical of recent writers in calling the opponents "syncretistic Jews infected with the Gnostic spirit"; but this opposition group, we must add, was within the Christian community or close enough to it to have heretical effects on the church, its Christology and life.

4. *Redating the New Testament* (Philadelphia: Westminster, 1976) 61-79. Bishop Robinson was particularly influenced by the views of Bo Reicke, as expressed, for example, in "The Historical Setting of Colossians," *Review and Expositor* 70 (1973) 429-38.

5. "The mighty acts of God" has become a way of referring to what God has done for the liberation of his people Israel, in the Hebrew Scriptures, and then, according to the New Testament, for his new community in Christ, the church. "God's mightiest act" would be, in the Old Testament, the deliverance from oppression in Egypt at the exodus; in the New Testament, God's raising Jesus from the dead.

6. While forgiveness is a common theme in the Old Testament (especially in cult), in the teachings of Jesus according to the Synoptic Gospels (especially in connection with healing miracles), and in the

Notes

preaching by the apostles in Acts, neither John's Gospel nor Paul employs the term very much. Paul talks of "iniquities forgiven" at Rom. 4:7 (as part of a rabbinic-style argument, quoting Ps. 32:1-2). The statement at Rom. 3:25, that God "passed over former sins," means God forgave such sins. Cf. R. Bultmann, *"aphiēmi"* and related words, in G. Kittel, ed., *Theological Dictionary of the New Testament* (Grand Rapids: Eerdmans), 1:511-12. If one asks why Paul spoke so little about forgiveness of sins, the likely answer is that he has a fuller and more precisely articulated system of thought where the content of forgiveness is conveyed by such terms as "justification" and "reconciliation." In particular, he regarded Christ's sacrifice on the cross as dealing with Sin not only in the past but also in the whole life and future existence of the believer. Colossians and Ephesians are therefore true to Paul's views elsewhere in mentioning forgiveness so little. (Col. 3:13 contains actually a different word than that translated "forgiveness" at 1:14.) The importance of 1:14 is that it links "redemption" as a theme with the common apostolic view about the "forgiveness of sins" at one's conversion or call to be a Christian, one's coming to faith by hearing the word of God and by Baptism. Cf. also H. Vorländer, "Forgiveness," in *The New International Dictionary of New Testament Theology*, ed. Colin Brown, vol. 1 (Grand Rapids: Zondervan, 1975) 701-702.

7. James D. G. Dunn, in his discussion of Col. 1:15-20 as an example of "Wisdom Christology" (where Jesus the Lord is spoken of in terms used in the Old Testament and elsewhere to portray Wisdom), remarks that any attempt in the first century, such as this hymn, to relate the exalted Lord to creation and to God's power and purpose for the world, "was almost bound to use the terminology of the then current philosophical speculation—not least the prepositions 'from,' 'in,' 'through' and 'for'— just as a Lutheran theologian today attempting to develop a particular view of the Lord's Supper is almost bound to use the prepositional formula 'in, with and under,' " but without pressing each little word, *Christology in the Making: A New Testament Inquiry into the Origins of the Doctrine of the Incarnation* (Philadelphia: Westminster, 1980) 187-94; quote on p. 193.

8. Most recent commentaries point out what seem parallels to phrases in these verses found in other religions of Paul's day. See, for example, Lohse, *Colossians and Philemon* 45-46, or Schweizer's *Colossians* 58, 64-65, 68, for such *religionsgeschichtlich* analogues. On the phrase "body (of Christ)," Schweizer's little book in the Chime Paperbacks series, *The Church as the Body of Christ* (Richmond, Va.: John Knox, 1964), esp. pp. 64-67, is a helpful distillation of research.

9. The phrase is used of Col. 1:15-20 by C. F. D. Moule, *The Epistles of Paul the Apostle to the Colossians and to Philemon* (New York: Cambridge University Press, 1957) 3 and 58, and by others because of the magnitude of what is said about Jesus Christ in these verses and because of the subsequent importance of the passage in the development of the church's Christology. On the latter point, Schweizer, *Colossians* 246-58, cf. also 259-77, presents numerous citations to show the importance of 1:15-20 from the second to the twentieth century.

10. Arius (ca. A.D. 250-336), a priest and deacon in Alexandria, taught that, while Christ was preexistent and had a role in creation, he was created by the Father out of nothing, and was designated as Son but was not "God" from all eternity. See Schweitzer, *Colossians* 250-52. The phrase at Col. 1:15*b* was interpreted by Arianism to mean that Christ was the first of God's creatures but a creature nonetheless. Theologians of more orthodox outlook argued that Christ, as "head of the church" (1:18*a*) and "first-born" (not "first-created"), was God incarnate, as in John 1:1-18. For some texts from the patristic discussion, see Richard A. Norris Jr., *The Christological Controversy* (Sources of Early Christian Thought, ed. William G. Rusch; Philadelphia: Fortress, 1980) 17-21, 83-101.

11. If our canonical Philippians was made up (perhaps between A.D. 80 and 95) from parts of three genuine letters (often identified as 4:10-20; chaps. 1–2; and 3:1ff.) and Colossians is modeled on this redacted product, we would then have an argument for dating Colossians even later. But some scholars use this similarity in structure with Philippians to argue that both Philippians and Colossians were written (at Paul's direction) during the same imprisonment (at Caesarea or Ephesus). Of course others may feel that the references to the false teachers in Colossians begin to appear more in the manner of 1 or 2 Corinthians than in the explosive way they do at Phil. 3:1.

12. Cf. Moule, *Colossians* 94-96, citing C. A. Anderson Scott; cf. also J. A. T. Robinson, *The Body: A Study in Pauline Theology* (SBT 5; London: SCM, 1952) 41-42. E. Schweizer, *Colossians* 142-43, is typical of commentators who are dubious about this interpretation, however, preferring a "spiritualized sense."

13. Cf. Moule, *Colossians* 97. The notion of a pact with the devil was common in patristic exegesis but is specifically rejected by exegetes today like Lohse, *Colossians and Philemon* 108 and n. 103, or Schweizer, *Colossians* 148.

14. Cf. Wesley Carr, "Two Notes on Colossians," *Journal of Theological Studies* 24 (1973) 492-96. The reference would then be to inscriptions, such as Paul and the Colossians might have seen at temple

sites, confessing some shortcoming by an adherent of the cult and mentioning punishment by the deity that brought about a sense of forgiveness. The details in this inscribed record stood as testimony against the wrongdoer. Carr develops the background further in his book, *Angels and Principalities: The Background, Meaning and Development of the Pauline Phrase hai archai kai hai exousiai* (SNTSMS 42; New York: Cambridge University Press, 1981) 55-58.

15. The combination "Christocentric" and "theoultimate" was a favorite of one of my seminary teachers in Philadelphia, Prof. Russell D. Snyder. If the New Testament centers in Jesus Christ and what has been accomplished and made known through him, it also is so arranged in its presentation that one can nevertheless not overlook its ultimate emphasis on God. At its highest Christological moments the New Testament ends up regularly with a reference to the Father's glory, name, or plan, as, for example, the closing note in Phil. 2:11 about "the glory of the Father" or in 2:9-11 what God has accomplished for Jesus, even after the high assertions about Christ in 2:6-8.

16. On "image," cf. C. F. D. Moule, *Man and Nature in the New Testament* (Facet Books, Biblical Series 17; Philadelphia: Fortress, 1967), esp. pp. viii-xvii, 1-4. Further, J. D. G. Dunn, *Christology in the Making* (cited above, n. 7) 105-107.

17. An alternative view, argued especially by John Knox in *Philemon among the Letters of Paul* (Nashville: Abingdon, 1959), holds that Philemon, overseer of the Christian churches in the Lycus Valley, lived in Laodicea with Apphia, his wife. Archippus, in whose house at Colossae the congregation there met, is said to be the owner of Onesimus. This view is rejected by Moule, *Colossians* 14-21, and by Lohse, *Colossians and Philemon* 175 and 186, among others. Decision on the role played by each person is important for theories about "the ministry" which Archippus is told to fulfill in Col. 4:17 (see below).

18. That the author of Luke-Acts wrote 1 and 2 Timothy and Titus is the contention of, among others, S. G. Wilson, *Luke and the Pastoral Epistles* (London: SPCK, 1979).

19. "The Epistle to the Laodiceans" is translated in Edgar Hennecke, *New Testament Apocrypha*, ed. Wilhelm Schneemelcher, trans. ed. R. McL. Wilson, vol. 2 (Philadelphia: Westminster, 1965) 128-32.

SELECTED BIBLIOGRAPHY

Burgess, Joseph. "The Letter to the Colossians," in J. P. Sampley, J. Burgess, G. Krodel, R. H. Fuller, *Ephesians, Colossians, 2 Thessalonians, The Pastoral Epistles.* Proclamation Commentaries. Philadelphia: Fortress, 1978. From analysis of the opponents, the hymn, eschatology, and other factors, the letter is determined to be pseudonymous and from Ephesus.

Gnilka, Joachim. *Der Kolosserbrief.* Herders Theologischer Kommentar zum Neuen Testament. Freiburg: Herder, 1980. A definitive commentary in German. From the Pauline school, in Ephesus, perhaps A.D. 70.

Houlden, J. L. *Paul's Letters from Prison: Philippians, Colossians, Philemon, and Ephesians.* Westminster Pelican Commentaries. Penguin Books, 1970; Philadelphia: Westminster, 1977. Likely by Paul from Ephesus, late 40s.

Johnston, George. *Ephesians, Philippians, Colossians, and Philemon.* Century Bible, New Edition. New York: Nelson, 1967. By Paul from Rome between 61 and 63.

Lightfoot, J. B. *Saint Paul's Epistles to the Colossians and to Philemon.* London: Macmillan, 1875; 7th ed., 1884, reprinted Grand Rapids: Zondervan. A venerable giant, still worth consulting. Argues that the Colossian opponents had affinities with the Essenes.

Lohse, Eduard. *Colossians and Philemon.* Trans. W. R. Poehlmann and R. J. Karris; ed. H. Koester. Hermeneia Commentary. Philadelphia: Fortress, 1971. By the Lutheran Bishop of

Hannover. A "theologian of the Pauline school" wrote Colossians about A.D. 80, with the letter's place in Pauline theology developed accordingly. Technical in details, using Greek (which, however, is always translated).

Martin, Ralph P. *Colossians: The Church's Lord and the Christian's Liberty.* Exeter: Paternoster Press, 1972. Idem, *Colossians and Philemon.* New Century Bible. London: Marshall, Morgan & Scott, 1974. Paul wrote from Ephesus at the time of Acts 19–20.

Moule, C. F. D. *The Epistles of Paul the Apostle to the Colossians and to Philemon.* The Cambridge Greek Testament Commentary. New York: Cambridge University Press, 1957. Defends Pauline authorship from Rome, A.D. 60. Valuable linguistic comments.

Rogers, Patrick V. *Colossians.* New Testament Message 15. Wilmington, Del.: Michael Glazier, 1980. Paul from Rome in 61.

Schweizer, Eduard. *The Letter to the Colossians.* Trans. A. Chester. Minneapolis: Augsburg, 1982. From Ephesus, perhaps by Timothy, in Paul's name, shortly after Philemon. Detailed notes; concern for the history of interpretation.

I have dealt with exegetical, hermeneutical, and ecumenical issues connected with Col. 1:15-20 in *Christ and Humanity*, ed. Ivar Asheim (Philadelphia: Fortress, 1970) 96-109; *Creation and New Creation: The Past, Present, and Future of God's Creative Activity* (Minneapolis: Augsburg, 1973) 42-56; and "Exegetes, Honesty and the Faith: Biblical Scholarship in Church School Theology," *Currents in Theology and Mission* 5 (1978) 16-32, especially pp. 21-22, 29-30.

The entire fall 1973 issue of *Review and Expositor* (70, 4) is devoted to articles on Colossians, including a section-by-section analysis.

ABOUT THE AUTHOR

John Reumann is a graduate of Muhlenberg College and the Lutheran Theological Seminary at Philadelphia. Ordained in 1950, he has organized mission congregations in New Jersey and Pennsylvania and has taught at the Philadelphia Seminary for more than thirty years, where he has also served as Dean and Acting President. His Ph.D. (classics, 1957) is from the University of Pennsylvania. He has done postdoctoral study at Cambridge and Göttingen Universities and taught in India and Israel. As editor, author, lecturer, and preacher, he is widely known, especially in ecumenical circles, including Catholic dialog, and for his work in the "Word and Witness" program.